IN QUEST OF
THE GOOD LIFE

Edwin R. Lincoln

IN QUEST OF THE GOOD LIFE

ISBN 0-89536-362-3

PRINTED IN U.S.A.

To the congregations at

Cheshire and Guilford, Connecticut

who finished these sermons by hearing them;

and to my wife who,

out of love,

listened to them twice.

Table of Contents

IV. The Great Commandments

Introduction

"Summertime, when the livin' is easy!" So goes the song from *Porgy and Bess*. While the "livin" may not be as easy as we would like it, at least summer is a bit more leisurely in the life of the church than that mad rush throughout the rest of the year.

Schedules are so tightly woven, and so many liturgical and parochial demands impinge upon the preacher week after week, he scarcely has time to develop consistent and orderly preaching themes. To be sure, the lectionary provides a framework. But even that is often interrupted by a special need demanding proclamation, or an urgent request from a board or committee that deserves sermonic treatment.

Developing themes through series of sermons is a satisfying practice for me. But it often turns to frustration because of the encroachment of the above. This is compounded when a pastor serves on a multiple staff. Rare is the opportunity to preach an extended series that builds to a climax, or allows adequate treatment of texts and themes — except in the summer!

Contrary to the wag who delights in saying that summer is the time when the lamp of Christendom burns low, this time of the year provides a wealth of opportunity to really work at your craft and offer some sound fruits of study and inspiration to people who are just as hungry for the Word as in other months, but have a little more time to chew on it.

Summer lets you dig into prophecy with a zest, develop themes on entire sections of the Bible, think about the Gospels as total books, or take a single text such as the great commandment and spend a month exploring the height, depth, and breadth of what it means to love God and neighbor.

And if ever the preacher wants a chance to have the congregation continue in fellowship and discussion after worship, summer is the time to pause with coffee, punch, or iced tea, and talk in an unhurried way about the experience of worship, or the content of the Word. Proclamation cries for response, and the preacher should be brave enough from time to time to hear it from the people. After all, God just heard his!

This book contains four sermon series for summer. Preparing and preaching them was a privilege. Rewriting them was a joy, for with each there flooded back memories of particular persons who were touched softly or sharply by them, and said so. And wonder of wonders — I had time to hear what they said. For a few moments each week we were that goodly fellowship who really cared about each other, because we knew that God really cared about us.

I.

The

Eighth

Century

Prophets

Amos
A Prophet in a Rage

Amos 5:4-24

I once asked a confirmation class what they thought a prophet was. Most of them said that a prophet was one who foretold the future. This is a common response from both young people and adults. In one sense, prophets do comment upon the future. They contemplate the past, observe the present, and then deduce the course of future events if there is no change of attitude or direction. All of us do that, more or less, in our own lives. We share this aspect of the prophetic stance.

But a prophet is more than that. Primarily, a prophet speaks for God. He is God's mouthpiece. He passes on the judgment and the joy of the Holy One who cares so much about his people that he wants to speak to them. If God did not care, he would be silent.

For the next few weeks, we are going to listen to four prophets who had a timely word for their day. They all lived during the eighth century B.C. They spoke at a time when the Hebrew people were relatively secure and self-satisfied. The nation was prosperous. The people were proud. But, often, prosperity and pride are purchased at the price of lost principle. What looked good on the outside was corrupt internally. God saw it and he sent his prophets to say it.

Amos, Hosea, Isaiah, and Micah come out of obscurity and challenge the nation's spiritual infidelity. Israel has broken faith with the mind of the Maker. The people have mismanaged their relationship with God and each other. These men cry out, "O Israel, this is not the way God wants you to be!"

These four prophets still speak for God today. Human beings still hate each other and themselves. What some may call the sick, sexy, and way-out songs and literature of our time may very well be both symptomatic of the psychotic state in which we find ourselves, and a protest that this is not what is intended for our lives. Young people read, listen to, and think deeply about these things. They know there is more to the world than feathering your nest. So do we. But perhaps the difference in the intensity of our concern is that while we stand to lose our life's work in the turmoil, they stand to lose their lives.

If ever a prophet were relevant to the world's convulsions, it is Amos. He is in a rage on behalf of God. He is angry because he understands that God loved the people, Israel, so much that he made a covenant of privilege and responsibility with them. They took the first part and forsook the second. They took the cash — "A little wine, a loaf of bread, and you by my side, baby!" — and let the moral and ethical credit go. They prostituted justice, twisted the commandments to their own desires, and covered the dignity of personhood with filth.

Amos witnessed bribery, theft, and adultery. He saw the temple of God turned into a slave block. He watched the ancient fertility gods being worshiped again. And then he saw the people go to worship, with hands folded, at the mainline United Church of Jahweh and try to drown out the stink of their society in the perfume of ritual. Thus, Amos cries out:

> I hate, I despise your feasts, and I take no delight in your solemn assemblies . . . Take away from me the noise of your songs; to the melody of your harps I will not listen. But let

*justice roll down like waters, and
righteousness like an ever-flowing stream.
(5:21, 23-24)*

Amos preached against the excesses of his day,
and in his own understanding, as a shepherd who
comes out of the wilderness and goes to the city.
There are not many happy verses in his book. He
could preach only judgment and destruction upon a
faithless people who turned the blessings of
prosperity into a curse through pride, callousness,
and indifference.

Now, before we brand Amos as a hopeless
dyspeptic who is long on criticism and short on
positive suggestions, it is absolutely essential to
understand the way the prophets teach. The Old
Testament prophets do not formulate doctrines, nor
do they build intellectual systems. They speak to
concrete situations that need immediate attention.
Their insights are partial and do not encompass the
full scope of God's truth. They begin a train of thought
which they cannot follow to its conclusion because of
the shortness of life. But others build upon them and,
through the work of many, God's truth is seen in all its
glory.

Also, it is important to understand the social and
economic tensions under which the eighth century
prophets, especially, labored. It was a tension
between the city and the country; the town and the
desert — between Cain, the sophisticated cereal-
maker, and Abel, the country-bumpkin sheep herder.
By and large, the prophets represented the life of the
desert where the faith of Israel was born. With the
growth of national government and urban society,
they saw the rigorous moral and spiritual ethic of the
desert God, Jahweh, slowly dissipated and
compromised in favor of money, power, and physical
excess. They saw the worth of people displaced by the

worth of possessions.

The natural reaction would be for these stern voices from the wilderness to call the people back to the desert, if they were to save their souls. In some instances, this emphasis is present. There were groups of people who refused to be caught up in the turmoil of the city and remained nomads in a developing nation. There is a parallel in our day with the Amish in Pennsylvania, and some back-to-nature communes.

While Amos would admire such groups for their devotion to their roots and for their moral fortitude, it is to his credit that he did not preach this solution to the Hebrew people. Even though he cried for a return to the ways of the God of their fathers, he did not counsel a return to the place where the father's bones were buried. That would make God dependent upon a particular form of social organization and limit him to one place. It would make it impossible for persons to meet God where they needed him most: in the city street and the suburban back yard.

Amos does not deny progress or condemn civilization. What he does condemn is the thinking that God has nothing to say to the contemporary situation. Nations may learn to fly to the moon, and yet forget to walk in the path of God's love. This is why Amos is so relevant to our life. He knows it is the business of religion to mold culture with meaning wherever people live, and that it must always be done with God as the architect.

Amos reminds us that God is not all sweetness and light. Those whom the Lord loves, he also disciplines. Those whom he chooses, of them he requires much. The day of the Lord may very well be a day of darkness, not light. Do we really know what we are asking for when we so glibly pray, "Thy kingdom come, thy will be done on earth"? Do we realize that we are asking for a reversal of our values, an upsetting of our priorities, and a breaking down of the comfortable barriers behind which we live? Amos does not believe we really want those things in the day of the Lord. Therefore, it will be a day of crisis and judgment.

The picture of God Amos gives to us is one of a Lord of all history and all people. This was a radical departure from the national consciousness of the Hebrew people who believed that their spiritual and patriotic stocks paid the highest dividends.

Unfortunately, this mood has characterized our own nation too often. Amos would be the first to say that we cannot dress up God in red, white, and blue bunting. God is not on the side of any one nation so it can make war with a good conscience. Amos would be the first to say that God does not look at our bank balance, the size of our house, the color of our skin, the sound of our voice, the variety in our liquor cabinet, or at our political allegiance as an estimate of our worth. He looks at our motives, our intentions, and our actions.

Amos would be the first to bring an indictment against the prostitution of knowledge which increases the efficiency with which we kill each other — subtly through pre-sweetened malnutrition, slowly with smog, or silently with nerve gas. Amos would most likely say the judgment of God rests upon the church when it hesitates to rock the ark, or sweep out the stalls once in a while by demanding justice and righteousness in human relationships.

He would wonder why Christians do not speak out more and say, "Every time you glorify war to your children and say a migrant worker is paid enough; every time you call another human being a 'nigger' or a 'spic', or dump your sewage into the river, you're wrong, man! You're breaking the heart of God; you're hanging Jesus up there on the cross again, and you're killing me and my kids! I can't keep quiet any more because you're a menace to the world and to the peace that passes all understanding."

Amos was thrown out of Bethel by the local bishop for saying something like that on the church steps. Amos was a prophet in a rage who spoke for his God whose love was spurned and whose truth was twisted. Somehow, you and I must begin to interpret God's intentions for his creation in concrete ways. Christians must speak for a God whose love was killed and whose truth was buried. The resurrection is always now.

Some years ago in a mid-western city, a college professor met a little boy outside the city museum. The professor asked the boy if he knew what was inside the building. The boy did not know. He had never been inside. The professor said that such a magnificent building should have a sign somewhere telling people what it was.

The lad immediately answered, "It does have a sign! See those big letters up there?"

Sure enough, there was an inscription over the portal which read, *AD GLORIAM MAGNI ARCHITECTI MUNDI ET HOMINUM FRATERNITATEM.*

The professor translated it out loud: "To the Glory of the Great Architect of the Universe and to Human Brotherhood."

"Does it really say that?" the boy asked in astonishment. "Just think, me with all my Latin and I couldn't read that sign."

"What do you mean 'With all your Latin'?" the professor asked.

"Why I know Latin," exclaimed the boy. And with his chest out and his arms at his side, he began to sing in a clear, soprano voice: "Gloria in excelsis deo; et in terra pax hominibus, Bonae voluntatis. Laudamus te,

Benedicimus te, Adoramus te . . ."

And on he went until the professor stopped him and said, "You do know Latin. Forgive me for doubting your word. It just goes to show how ignorant some of us grown-ups are."

When the two of them parted, the professor heard the little boy mumble to himself as he walked away, "Me with all my Latin and I couldn't read that sign."

What about us with all our Latin — with all our technical and economic resources — with all our wizard machines and fabulous knowledge stretching from the sub-atomic electron out beyond the Milky Way. We still cannot read that sign very well: "To the Glory of the Great Architect of the Universe and to Human Brotherhood." With all our learning, justice and equity do not run through the rivers of life. With all our learning, we have not learned to love each other.

Amos could see no alternative on the part of God except the destruction of a faithless people. But we have seen Christ. He is God's alternative. Christ is in the world, calling us to join him in the struggle for justice, love, and peace. God works out his purpose in the crucible of human history. Our task is to join him and help the world, through our own lives, to read that sign, "To the Glory of the Great Architect of the Universe and to Human Brotherhood," while there is still a sign to read.

Hosea
His Grief Became His Gospel

Hosea 11:1-9

In this series we are examining the ministry and message of four eighth century, Old Testament prophets: Amos, Hosea, Isaiah, and Micah. They lived in a period of great prosperity. The land of Canaan was well settled and cultivated. Cities began to grow through commerce. The monarchy was firmly established. Even though Palestine was divided into two kingdoms, there was reasonable communication and concord between them.

However, with prosperity, moral and spiritual decay began to set in. In the northern kingdom, especially, money and power were coveted. Possessions took precedence over people. The gathering thunderheads of international conflict went unseen by a people in search of the next sensation. Assyria and Egypt were rattling their swords and looking at Israel as the best place to play their game of war. But a little money here, a little treaty there, seemed to quiet down their growling.

The prophet Amos cried out against these distortions in his society and tried to call the people back to the stern righteousness of their God. He denounced the double life of those who prayed together on Sunday, and then plotted against one another on Monday. All the organized religion in the world was useless if you let your spiritual tackle hang loose in your dealings with your neighbor. God wanted justice and righteousness from his people, not songs and incense. And since they were not willing to buy such a bill of goods, Amos' message was ultimately one of judgment and the disintegration of the nation.

Hosea sounds a different note in his ministry. The strains of judgment and national turmoil are still present in his words, but he takes the gemstone of God's truth from Amos and turns it over, discovering that on the other side of judgment there is grace. We must remember that the insights of the prophets are partial. They build upon each other in their struggle to speak for God. Each has a metered word for his time. All their words together point to the Word made flesh, Christ Jesus, who brings us here this morning.

Hosea's message grows out of a personal tragedy in his own life. His grief became his gospel. He was married to a woman called Gomer. They had three children; two sons and a daughter. Gomer became a prostitute in the nearby city of Bethel, the same city where a short time earlier Amos had delivered his message of doom. Maybe she couldn't stand it down on the farm any more. Maybe the city made her too many glowing promises. Maybe she couldn't stand Hosea any more, and their love lost its luster, becoming a gray thing.

In any event, this was the circumstance. All the imploring of Hosea and the children could not make her return. Hosea was grief-stricken. I suppose he got mad, too. Perhaps he considered writing a bill of divorce which was the right of the Hebrew husband and to which his wife would have no recourse. The important thing is he did not do this. He must have searched his soul for an answer to this tragedy, and laid awake many nights searching for the meaning of love, trust, and forgiveness. I imagine he weighed his own complicity in this event and tried to find a way to redeem the situation.

Well, a solution presented itself in a way that I

don't think Hosea planned at all. Gomer's beauty and charms slowly faded away. With each lover, she lost a bit of her soul, trying desperately to give it in love, and having it wrenched from her in selfish passion instead. The body fades quickly when violence is done to the soul. Gomer was no longer sought after by the men of the city. She no longer received "little cakes of raisins" as an inducement to give of her charms. She became frantic as her money disappeared, her food deteriorated, and her bed too often became a dark corner in some garbage-filled alley.

Gomer became so desperate that she sold herself into slavery. Hosea, on one of his frequent trips to Bethel to search for his wife, found her on the slave block in the market place. He bought her back for fifteen pieces of silver and a basket of barley, saying, "Come home with me and dwell as mine for many days; do not play the harlot any more, or belong to another man; so will I also be to you." (3:2-3)

Now, if Hosea were trying to be a good fellow by saying, "I will forgive and forget;" or thinking, "Well, I've had my fling and she was entitled to hers;" or if he were performing some perverted public act of unctuous righteousness designed to punish Gomer by announcing, "See how good I am and how wicked you have been," then his action would be demonic.

I suspect that Hosea viewed his act of purchase in the market-place in the most uncomplicated of terms. He simply said to his wife, "I loved you, I still love you, and I want to live with you and have you with me. I don't know whether you still love me, and I can't make you love me again. I can only respond to the way my emotions guide me, and that is to bring you back and see if we can make a go of it."

We don't know how their marriage worked out after that. It surely took a lot of work to put it in balance again. We do not know what happened to their marriage, but we do know what happened to Hosea. He reflected upon the trouble in his own household and saw in it a corollary between God and the people, Israel. He asked himself, "Is this the way God deals with his people who leave his household and go whoring after other gods? Does God weep when his covenant is broken, and does forgiveness mean not to forget, but rather to say, 'Whatever has happened between us shall not separate us'?"

Hosea reflected upon these things and took a step beyond Amos in presenting the nature of God. Amos' indictment is provoked by man's inhumanity to man (and that must never be forgotten), but Hosea's passion is kindled by Israel's unfaithfulness to God. Hosea is not satisfied to deal with external rules of conduct; he must search out the secret feelings by which actions are prompted. We might say Amos is extensive while Hosea is intensive. Amos is a preacher to the conscience, and such men are not necessarily preachers of repentance. Hosea is a preacher to the agony of the soul and finds a basis for hope in the love of God and the repentance of the people.

So, when God speaks in Hosea, we hear a deity torn apart by mixed emotions. At one moment God reflects upon his love for Israel:

When Israel was a child, I loved him, and out of Egypt I called my son . . . I took them up in my arms, I led them with cords of compassion, with the bands of love . . . and I bent down to them and fed them. (11:1-4)

And then in the next breath, God's anger overwhelms him and he cries out:

They shall return to the land of Egypt, and Assyria shall be their king . . . The sword shall rage against their cities . . . and devour them in their fortresses. (11:5-6)

But a love that not even God can push aside presses in and says again:

How can I give you up, O Ephraim! How can I hand you over, O Israel! . . . My heart recoils within me . . . I will not come to destroy. (11:8-9)

Throughout the book, this tension that exists within God himself never seems to be resolved. But the fact that it is there — the tension between judgment and grace, between vengeful anger and forgiveness, between hate and love — is an encouragement to never utterly despair.

Those who hear the message of Hosea, and act upon it, must be willing to be labeled as odd people. The world does not pay much dividend for acceptance, understanding, and forgiveness. It often rejects such actions as impractical. And yet it wonders about the source from which such actions spring.

I remember hearing a story about a Korean Christian pastor who served a tiny, broken-down church in the town of Soon Chen. He had two sons. On one occasion he shared his concern with them about the future of his parish.

"My sons, why is it that so few come to worship?"

One son replied, "Father, the Korean people cannot believe this new gospel. It is not part of our heritage that one can forgive as did Jesus. I guess we must show them the way."

A few weeks later, a band of robbers attacked the little town and murdered the pastor's two sons. The police found the killer and he made a complete confession of the crime. He was tried, found guilty, and sentenced to death. The father of the murdered boys stood up in the courtroom and asked permission to speak:

"Honorable judge, I forgive this man who killed my sons. By sentencing the killer of my beloved ones to death, the law may satisfy justice, but does nothing to help my grief. Why kill him, then? Why not give him to me? Let me bring him into my family. He can take the place of one of those I have lost. If you will let me have him, I promise Almighty God to treat him as my own son."

Those present could not believe their ears or their eyes when they saw the father put his hand upon the murderer's shoulder and smile at him.

Of course, we believe it would be foolish to release a killer into the custody of such naive hands as those of the gentle pastor. And of course, Hosea was being a foolish romantic who would only find grief again in his decision for reconciliation with his wife.

But once you see a person engage in the unpredictable and the unimaginable, you cannot forget it. No matter how hard you try, it steals in upon you and makes you consider God's ways with his people. What a horrible, hopeless world this would be if there were never any acts such as these to brighten our human history. What a desolate climate we would inhabit if there were never a radical act of love.

Hosea believed that God was a god of love and forgiveness. To be sure, the fortunes of Israel were sliding downhill. To be sure, the national conscience was rotten to the core, and every kind of perversion was practiced. But Hosea was convinced that if you cut yourself off from God, you cut yourself off from other people, and then you felt you had to drown your collective guilts in acts of rage, fear and exploitation. But the almighty God, the jealous God whose love is spurned, the God who hates the sin of his people and executes wrath and judgment, the God who never lets you off, is also the God who wears his heart on his shirtsleeve and never lets you go.

In the play, *Green Pastures*, by Marc Connelly, the Lord was always on the verge of putting an end to his creation. He would go down to earth in hope, and then become sick at heart when he saw how humans treated each other. Each time he would almost give Gabriel a chance to blow his judgment horn.

Now, outside the Lord's office in heaven, a shadowy figure paces up and down. The Lord asks Gabriel who that fellow is outside the door. Gabriel answers that it is a prophet from the planet earth, and he wants to make a plea for his people. He always looks sad and grief-stricken, but he's got a faith of hope and trust, too. He's been walking out there for years.

Well, the Lord was too upset to see Hosea. He had his prodigal earth on his mind. He decides to go down to earth one last time and give it a final chance to repent. This time the Lord meets a soldier who is defending the Holy City with his life. He asks him if he is a believer. The soldier answers that he is, for he worships the God of Hosea. This Lord is a God of forgiveness and patience, of mercy and love, not revenge.

The Lord goes back to his office in heaven. His heart is heavy and confused. He wants to see this Hosea. But Hosea is no longer there. Instead, the Lord hears voices coming up from earth. He looks down and sees a man being taunted as he hangs upon a cross. And then he hears the man's cry pounding in his ears. While the play does not tell us what the cry is, it surely must have been, "Father, forgive them, for they know not what they do!"

The book of the prophet Hosea is the closest to the Christian gospel that we find in the Old Testament. Hosea was a man ahead of his time. And so were Christ, and Gandhi, and Martin Luther King, and the Korean pastor. They all practiced the foolishness of faith and the impracticalities of forgiveness in the face of the hard realities of the world. The landscape of history is dotted with men and women ahead of their time. They keep hope and meaning alive for us.

Christians should be ahead of their time, planning the impractical and pursuing the impossible. Christians should be ahead of their time accepting the unacceptable and listening to the unbearable. The gospel does not ask us to embrace other people's sins; only other people. It asks us to be willing to get our fingers burned, or to be played for a fool sometimes so that the river of love and forgiveness does not get clogged up with suspicion, fear, and indifference.

Whenever I am feeling down, I take out some pictures I have saved, pictures of persons who have lived as people ahead of their times. They represent a picture of God that keeps me from despair. God must have his picture book, too. And I am sure he has a picture of Hosea in it. Hosea is one of God's pictures of us that keeps him from despair.

Isaiah
Prophet of Faith

Isaiah 6:1-12, 7:3-17

The eighth century prophets are speaking to us this month. They are Amos, Hosea, Isaiah, and Micah. These four are not the first to bear the name of prophet in Israel's history. They are, however, the first to present a systematic, literate exposition of the way God deals with his people, and how the people must respond to God so that the covenant between God and Israel will not be broken.

We have seen Amos raging against injustice and unrighteousness committed by a people who lived as if God did not exist. His verdict was judgment, dissolution, and destruction.

We have seen Hosea mourning over the infidelity of a people who lived as if God were impotent. His verdict also was judgment. But through it he sees a tenacious forgiveness of a God who, though he may not let you off, will, at the same time, neither let you go.

The prophet Isaiah adds a new dimension to the divine-human relationship, the dimension of faith. This prophet is the first in a succession of Isaiahs whose words have been compiled in one volume that bears that name. The book of the prophet Isaiah bears the mark of at least three writers, and possibly more, spanning a period of at least 200 years. The Isaiah of the eighth century has given us approximately the first two-thirds of the book. The remainder of the prophecy, though not written by him, builds upon his pioneering spirit.

Seen as a whole, it is a book of great joy. Yet, the prophet, Isaiah was not a joyful man. Only those who come after him make the book that way. But also, only because he laid the foundation for the challenge and demands of faith, could they make it that way.

Our Isaiah lived in Jerusalem in the kingdom of Judah and began his ministry in 740 B.C. We know the date because he tells us that "In the year that king Uzziah died, I saw the Lord . . . I heard his voice . . . and I was sent."

Unlike Amos and Hosea who came from the rural countryside, Isaiah came from the city. Unlike Amos and Hosea who appeared out of nowhere — who blew in, blew up, and blew out — Isaiah ministered to those he knew all his life. Unlike Amos and Hosea who were uncut, unknown gems, caring little about public relations and process planning, Isaiah was an aristocrat, a polished statesman, and a friend of those in high places.

His call to be a prophet was born out of trauma, not on the intensely personal level that Hosea experienced, but on a national level when a tragedy shakes the psychic foundations of an entire people so that nothing seems stable anymore. The economic heart begins to fibrillate, and anxiety makes the social mind stagger about in vertigo. The death of king Uzziah was such a tragedy.

He had ruled for fifty years, stabilized and protected his nation, and caused it to prosper. Yet, he died of leprosy! To die from this disease was a sign of unfaithfulness and sin. Yet how could this be? Uzziah had served his country well.

"Seek the answer in worship," the troubled spirit says. And it is in worship that Isaiah finds the answer, not to his king's unseemly death, but to the future course of his own life. In the temple, this devout man received the mantle of prophecy.

Now, this did not happen to every one in Judah. Prosperity and complacency often share the same bed. The nation waxed fat and dozed at noonday. God's in his heaven and all is well in Judah. A king dies and a nation must mourn, not for the king, but for themselves. The king's passing marks the wearing off of the anesthesia of delusion. The shallow roots of affluence are laid bare. Now the people must reflect upon the fact that this death may signal the first stages of their own death. They are shocked at the disease because it is their own. Not many can face it. Such anxiety is too much to bear.

So, mourn quickly and violently! Fill the temple with the smoke of many sacrifices! Beat your breasts until they are bruised, and wail until you are exhausted! For a while, you cast the demon out of yourself. For a while, your guilt reels before the onslaught of your devotion. And then, go back to your vineyard, back to your work, back to your house, back to the solid and substantial things and say, "Now I must forget; now everything will be all right. The disease is conquered. The king is dead. The expiation has been accomplished. Everything will be all right — until the next time?"

Not many can face prolonged reflection upon themselves which the death of another causes. Those few who can set their course for great agony and travail of the spirit. Isaiah was one who reflected and heard the truth. King Uzziah was not the only one who was unclean. So was Isaiah; so was the nation. They were unclean through the practice of misplaced faith, soiled by complacent and self-assured piety. Here was a people who had faith in everything — the future, the weather, the stock market, the priests, the army, the king — everything but God. A proper people, a religious people, a believing people, but not a faithful people.

Isaiah's major contribution is the bridge of faith he throws across the tension gap between Amos' message of judgment and Hosea's message of forgiveness. Faith is what God wants from his people. Their appropriation and execution of it is the path of righteousness.

Now, faith has a special meaning for Isaiah. The prophets used two words for faith. The first is the "faith that believes." This kind of faith is legitimate and necessary as a foundation in the religious quest. In the seventh chapter, Isaiah warns King Ahaz not to make alliances with governments in order to insure protection against Egypt and Assyria. There is no permanent protection in an alliance on earth unless the people first have an alliance with God. Ahaz is urged to seek a sign from God to this effect. But Ahaz refuses, saying he will not put God to the test. He has confidence in the Lord his God; he has the "faith that believes."

Isaiah certainly would commend Ahaz for his pious expression. Yet, the prophet still predicts the downfall of the nation, for the "faith that believes" is not enough. The people must have the second kind of faith; the "faith that acts," the faith that redresses wrong-doing, and confirms the "faith that believes."

Isaiah emphasizes this kind of faith to his people. He always uses this word along with such words as justice, constancy, truth, and equity. In one sense, he is saying to his people, "You are so religious. You are so proper and enthusiastic about your place of favor in the family of nations. Your forms are flawless. You know when to bow, when to salute, when to take off your hat, when to clap and laugh and cry. Prophets before and after me have told and will tell you that to believe is pious and God rewards such piety. But in the far perspective of faith there is no hiding place for favorites. Faith in God is not vision alone. No, faith is vision plus valor; the vision to see the constancy and faithfulness of God — to see the intent of the Creator for his creation — and then the valor to act upon the vision in the life you live so that others can share what you have seen."

Isaiah did not win this battle he fought for his people's minds and spirits. The "faith that acts" was too hard for those who "took their ease in Zion." Later prophets would take up this theme, and finally Jesus of Nazareth. What Isaiah did begin was the idea that man and God were in a partnership; that together they had a mission to seek and to save the lost. Isaiah learned that God did not choose to engage in this enterprise alone.

When Isaiah confronts the Holy One in his vision in the temple, God does not do anything in the physically active sense. He just talks. In the vision God asks, "Whom shall I send, and who will go for us?"

Isaiah responds, "Here I am! Send me."

This response, however, is timeless. It is not confined to Isaiah alone. It is also for you and me to make, in our visions and in our contemporary temples. Davie Napier makes this very clear in his book, *A Time For Burning:*

It is the year that King Uzziah died.
That's any year — for kings, my friend, are
dying:
since any child of man is child of God,
born to be free, and to subdue the earth.
My God, we go on killing kings like flies;
potential kings, the little kids that perish,
puking away their short-lived animation;
starved or exposed; or caught by rampant wars
imposed by men who would be emperors,
restraining other men from exercising
their given right to live as kings, as men.

This is the year of King Uzziah's death,
and these are times when kingliness is
    crushed,
when man, conceived to be a little less
than God, is less than man. This is a time
of shaking of foundations — and a time
of burning.

These are the awful days of dying kings,
when men, born to be men, are less than men.
The sacrificial altar fire is burning.
Foundations shake. And we are all unclean.
But if we listen with prophetic ears,
within the smoke-filled temple of our world
the seraphim are calling, burning calls
to burning, strangely not of death but life,
not of despair, but hope, and not of shame
but glory. Burning cries of holiness,
invading all of man's unholiness,
as Christ, the son of God, the son of man,
the king — unceasingly invading time,
incessantly enduring crucifixion —
proclaims the ultimate but, in a sense,
already present rule of righteousness.

If you are burned by burning, intimate
with altar fires; if your own lips are seared
with burning coals from sacrificial altars;
if crucifixion — once for all in Christ
or in the bloody stream of human history —
if crucifixion of the son of man
fully impinges on your consciousness,
then you will not be able to escape
the Calling of the Caller; you will know
that you are called, called irresistibly,
without a word of promise of success;
called out against insuperable odds

to go and speak and work and live, in faith
that judgment must be finally redemptive,
that fire ultimately purifies,
that burning is for cleansing and forgiveness,
that love and righteousness and holiness
in fact pervade this shattered habitation.

And you and I are called to live in love
and affirmation of a burning world,
in confidence that corporate guilt is purged,
our corporate want of cleanness is forgiven;
that even if the smoke is never cleared
a Holiness invades our wanton violence
and Glory fills the anguish of our times.

The year that King Uzziah died: a time
of burning, time of shaking, time of calling.
"Whom shall I send and who will go for us?"
And I say, trembling like a slender reed
before the hurricane, in hope alone
of love and affirmation, confidence —
I say, "I think I'm here. Send me."*

*Reprinted with permission of The Pilgrim Press, from Time of Burning by B. Davie Napier. Copyright © 1970 United Church Press.

Micah
This is True Religion

Micah 6:1-8

The holy fathers who gathered our Bible together into one book made an unfortunate distinction between major and minor prophets on the basis of verbiage rather than value. Whoever wrote the most words was called a major prophet. Whoever followed the dictum that brevity is the soul of wit was classified as a minor prophet. Micah falls into the second category.

This state of affairs is regrettable, for it causes many people to miss the mountain-top experiences of prophecy which so often come from the little man, the unknown man, who walks unseen through life. The eighth century prophet Micah was such a man. His words are few, but his insights are many. He is one of those giants who puts great thoughts in few words.

We know very little about Micah. He was a contemporary of Isaiah, and he lived in the country near Jerusalem. Yet, there is no evidence that he and Isaiah ever met. We know he spoke publicly at the close of the eighth century when the kingdom of Judah and the city of Jerusalem stood alone before the military might of Assyria. The northern kingdom had fallen. The prophecies of Amos against the city of Bethel were confirmed. All the surrounding nations had been overrun.

When you compare Isaiah and Micah, you discover they are alike only in their fundamental faith, but poles apart in their interpretation of it and its application to life. These two prophets represent two different social levels. Isaiah is an aristocrat; Micah is a democrat. Isaiah is a friend of kings and princes; Micah associates with the common people. Isaiah lives in Jerusalem and considers the capital to be the hub of the universe; Micah lives on the land and has as little regard for the infallibility of Jerusalem as a mid-western farmer has for Washington, D.C. Isaiah is concerned primarily with politics and international affairs, while Micah does not pass beyond ethical and religious considerations.

Over the years, Micah has suffered in comparison to his great contemporary, Isaiah. I guess we are more interested in capitals and kings, presidents and generals than in country people, slum dwellers, and production workers. After all, you can't have everybody on your mind. But everybody can have somebody on their minds, and Micah believed that somebody had to have the nobodies on his mind.

The occasion of his ministry was a simple and cruel fact: redevelopment. The city of Jerusalem 2700 years ago had its landlords, its mortgage holders, its politicians and bankers. The land they held and the people they controlled were mere statistics on a clay tablet. They began to eye the countryside as a place for a second home. In order to get the land, you had to move the farmers out. So, mortgages were called, eviction notices served, and crops plowed under. This is what Micah saw:

They covet fields and seize them; and houses, and take them away; they oppress a man and his house, a man and his inheritance . . . (Micah 2:2)

But you rise against my people as an enemy; you strip the robe from the peaceful, from those who pass by trustingly with no thought of war. The women of my people you drive out

*from their pleasant houses; from their young
children you take away my glory forever.
(Micah 2:8-9)*

*Is it not for you to know justice? — you who
hate the good and love the evil; who tear the
skin from off my people, and their flesh from
their bones; who eat the flesh of my people,
and flay their skin from off them, and break
their bones in pieces, and chop them up like
meat in a kettle, like flesh in a caldron. (Micah
3:1b-3)*

Undoubtedly, all this was done within the bounds
of the law of the land, but not the law of the soul.
Micah reads like an ancient *Grapes of Wrath*. Perhaps
Steinbeck researched him for his book. Micah cannot
understand why a man would treat another in this
way. He cannot remain silent. Unlike Amos who was
only a spectator to the abuses he denounced, Micah
felt these things in his own body. Micah speaks
strongly because he feels strongly. Perhaps he was a
victim himself of the great land grab. He becomes a
spokesman for his inarticulate friends. And in his
speaking, an answer forms as to why people practice
evil against each other, and what can be done about
it.

Part of his answer revolves around his opinion of
the city, Jerusalem. Micah parts ways with the
movement of prophecy up to this point by refusing to
regard Jerusalem as a supremely holy city which
should be spared the horrors of war as if God has
thrown up some spiritual shield around it. Jerusalem
is just as liable to judgment, dissolution, and
destruction as any other human community.
Jerusalem has the same seeds of evil in it as any other
city. In fact, it may have more because its residents
think they dwell under divine amnesty in the shadow

of the temple, and need not be as alert to the cries of a neighbor in a less-favored locale.

It is so much easier for me to get a credit card in a department store when I say I am from Guilford, than if I were from Congress Avenue in New Haven and was black or Puerto Rican. And yet, my location says little about my integrity or willingness to pay. From Micah's point of view, Jerusalem's location as the dwelling-place for God's name said little about the righteousness of the people who lived there.

Micah might even go so far as to say that the religion of Jerusalem is an "opiate of the people," if the ceremonies associated with worship — the fires, the holy oils, the chants, and the splendid architecture — are the ultimately satisfying things and lull the participant into a false sense of well-being. True religion should not produce the peace of self-satisfaction, but should precipitate the disturbing peace of involvement with the needs of the world. In fact, those who worship must first recognize that they, too, are a people in need — in need of relationship, in need of love, and in need of the impulse to serve, help, and heal.

God does not require the worship of temple and church to make him happy. People need these things because they are impelled to articulate the inexpressible and touch, however briefly, the divine that is in their midst — the divine that gets lost in frenzied activity. Worship is a delight to God insofar as it advances his intentions of growth and love for his creation. Short of that it is irrelevant and an affront.

I don't imagine Micah went to church very often, but he knew the religious history of his people and the stern demands of his God. He knew the meaning of a covenant. He gives us the essence of true religion and states the intentions of God in a few words and earns a place in the hall of history's spiritual giants:

He has showed you, O man, what is good; and what does the Lord require of you but to do justice, and to love kindness, and to walk humbly with your God? (Micah 6:8)

Micah blends the justice of Amos, the mercy of Hosea, and the faith of Isaiah into a single path. He does not put God first in his formula, lest he encourage the pious person to stop there in his religious search. His first two injunctions pertain to man's relationship to man. God requires justice — the recognition of every person's right, and the discharge of every duty in such a way that it brings health and well-being to the whole community. God requires mercy or kindness, which is the essential part of justice and fills it with the joy of forgiveness. And God requires humility — the renunciation of all human arrogance and selfish will. It is an active waiting in confidence to hear what God, the Lord and King of the universe, will direct. John the Elder, in the New Testament, drank deeply from the spring of this prophet's insight when he wrote:

If anyone says, "I love God," and hates his brother, he is a liar; for he who does not love his brother whom he has seen, cannot love God whom he has not seen. (1 John 4:20)

Micah tells it like it is. A religion which is merely an emotional palliative and does not issue in creative conduct between human beings is no religion at all. It is a sin against the very God who made a covenant with us to create a society wherein "they shall sit every man under his vine and under his fig tree, and none shall make them afraid." (Micah 4:4)

Micah is not a perfect person. He has his social and economic blind spots. His bias, like ours, is born out of his geographical and vocational location. But he has a vision that goes beyond his human limitations and if we lose it, we are doomed. He has a vision of a savior.

He speaks of one who is to come as an instrument and agent of God. And he believes that this one representative man — this one real man — would come, not from the Jerusalems of notoriety, but from the Bethlehems of obscurity. This one would come out of nowhere and convict the souls of people everywhere. He would be credible to the common, ordinary people of the world (which we are), for he would be one of them and share their sorrows and their joys. These are Micah's words which we read in the Advent season in the church:

> But you, O Bethlehem . . . who are little to be among the clans of Judah, from you shall come forth for me one who is to be ruler in Israel, whose origin is from of old, from ancient days . . . And he shall stand and feed his flock in the strength of the Lord, in the majesty of the name of the Lord his God. And they shall be secure, for now he shall be great to the ends of the earth. (Micah 5:2-4)

Micah not only dreamed God's dreams for his people; he also gave voice to them. He teaches us that true religion is not in proper ritual, but in right conduct with each other. God does not look more favorably upon wealth, power, and prestige, nor does he free those so endowed from responsibility toward the less fortunate.

Yet, God lets none of his people go entirely. He is a persistent God, ever devising new ways to be heard, even to the point of using a carpenter to speak for him. And why this persistence? Because he wants to put back together those scattered words of "It is good" which he spoke with a smile on the morning of creation, and which the disobedience of man shattered with a scream of hate. God persists in order to bring to pass that crazy, way-out dream which he and some of his people keep reminding us of time and time again. Both Isaiah and Micah quote an earlier oracle spelling out this dream. I leave it with you in the beautiful phrases of Scottish metrical verse:

No strife shall rage, nor hostile feuds
    disturb those peaceful years;
To ploughshares men shall beat their swords
    to pruninghooks their spears.
No longer hosts encountering hosts
    shall crowds of slain deplore;
They hang the trumpet in the hall,
    and study war no more. (Micah 4:3)

II.

The

Wisdom

Literature

Ecclesiastes
The Saddest Man

Ecclesiastes 1:1-18

This morning I wish to begin a short series of sermons on three books in the Old Testament: Ecclesiastes, Proverbs, and Job. This literature belongs to what is called the wisdom school of Israel. The prophet Jeremiah speaks of those who are the leaders of the people. He names the prophet, the priest, and the wise man. These three groups molded, preserved, and popularized the religious heritage of Israel. Each depended upon the other, even though like labor, management, and capital in our own society, there was a good deal of tension between them.

The wise men felt that the common folk of society did not receive an adequate ministry from the prophets and the priests. The prophet dealt with impossible ideals, and the priests turned those ideals into oppressive practices, but no one seemed to "tell it like it is." No one seemed to understand that the man on the street had some problems which organized religion did not touch. The wise men tried to fill this vacuum.

Now, whether they did a good or bad job in filling the vacuum, the wisdom school deals with important questions such as, "Is there any meaning to life?" "How can I get by day by day?" "Why does an innocent person suffer?" Because of questions like these, the wisdom writings are worth looking at in the light of Jesus Christ.

The book Ecclesiastes had a stormy journey before

it became part of our Bible. Because of its pessimistic message, there was a long controversy over whether or not it should be included. It was finally admitted to the Scriptures, not on religious grounds, but because of a pseudonymn which suggested that King Solomon was the author.

The man who wrote Ecclesiastes was called the "Preacher." He must have chuckled at that title, for what he says tends to empty churches rather than encourage people to worship. Ecclesiastes does not inspire the reader to faith. It is pessimistic in its tone and fatalistic in its thought. The writer sees little sense to life other than seizing the moment for what pleasure there may be in it. He does not give that moment any eternal significance.

The Preacher claims to have tasted a bit of everything in life. He says that all his days have been spent in testing life to see if it means anything. His conclusion is stated in his opening words:

Vanity of vanities, says the Preacher,
vanity of vanities! All is vanity. (Ecclesiastes 1:2)

Like some ancient Omar Khayyam, he looks out upon the world and declares that human beings are:

But helpless Pieces of the Game He (God) plays
Upon this Chequer-board of Nights and Days;
Hither and thither moves, and checks, and slays,
And one by one back in the Closet lays.

Not once does the Preacher use the personal name for God. And only once does he refer to the religious community of the people of Israel. You hear a wistful sigh over the idea of a personal God who desires fellowship with his beloved Israel. You hear a sigh over the idea of a God who is a present help in trouble, or to whom you can pray. The god of the Preacher is creator only — of both good and evil —

who pulled the string to start the spinning top and then withdrew to more important matters:

> A generation goes, and a generation comes, but the earth remains forever. The sun rises and the sun goes down, and hastens to the place where it rises. The wind blows to the south, and goes round to the north; round and round goes the wind, and on its circuits the wind returns. All streams run to the sea, but the sea is not full; . . . What has been is what will be, and what has been done is what will be done; and there is nothing new under the sun.
> (Ecclesiastes 1:4-7a, 9)

The hopeless, faithless, joyless book of Ecclesiastes points to the caprice of the natural world and the inadequacy of human ideals and efforts to cope with its whims.

But when I begin to question why this book ever got into the Bible, I have to admit that this dismal and moody gentleman talks about a part of all of us who share his moments of skepticism and despair. Sometimes, life does seem like a cruel joke. Sometimes, it does look like vanity and a chasing after a flimsy bubble.

There is a negative attractiveness in the writing of the Preacher. He does not tell lies. He is honest about his observations. You read his words and say, "That's right! I've seen that, too!"

When he beats out his rhythm of opposites, you begin to nod your head in agreement with the cadence they measure:

> a time to be born, and a time to die;
> a time to plant, and a time to pluck up what
>   is planted;
> a time to kill, and a time to heal;
> a time to break down, and a time to build up;
> a time to weep, and a time to laugh;

a time to mourn, and a time to dance . . .
(Ecclesiastes 3:2-4)

So what's wrong with good timing, we say. It helps you catch the tide of opportunity. Good timing prevents a waste of effort on things which, for the moment, cannot be done.

And when the Preacher says he has seen the strong oppress the weak, or the wicked and foolish sitting in high places, we know that these inequities are part of our experience, too. Innocent people do suffer indignities at the hands of fools and sadists. We know that the status quo is a powerful tool for crushing an adventuresome spirit. The Preacher would have looked at the news photos of VietNam refugees, or of fighting in Angola, and said, "You see, I'm right. The sad music of senseless sorrow and suffering plagues your world, too. All is vanity and a chasing after a bubble."

The Preacher is so right about so many things — so honest in his sensory observations — that it is easy to believe he is right about his conclusions — that life is a game of dice, a waste of time, and an unhappy business.

But wait a minute, now! We're here today as followers of Jesus Christ whose word is a hopeful and a healing one. That being the case, we must announce that the preacher is not right in his conclusions. He set for himself the goal of testing everything under the sun, and found no evidence of the providence, love, and mercy of God. I think the Preacher was a sick man. He suffered from many diseases of the spirit which are contagious. I'll mention two of them this morning.

First, the Preacher had a strong mind, but he had a weak heart. He knew how to observe and report the truth of fact, but he had no understanding of the truth of feeling. He had no capacity for either faith or trust in God or people. He would look out on the congregation this morning and say, "Here is the biggest collection of meanness, anger, jealousy, hatred, prejudice, and greed you'll ever hope to see!"

Now, he is probably stating a fact about our contrary natures, but because he has no depth of feeling, no sense of the unseen — because he has a weak heart — he does not understand the needs that well up inside us for forgiveness, acceptance, and love. He does not see that we are capable of mercy and sacrifice. He does not understand that our coming here is a faith-judgment in a loving God who has the power to transform life, and that the invisible can often be more real than what is seen on the surface. The Preacher will not enter this church to worship. He will only come to observe and report.

And second, the Preacher also suffers from "I" trouble. The personal pronoun "I" dominates his thinking. His life is centered upon himself, and he never gets beyond himself. The Preacher is his own worst enemy. He does a good job of reporting evil and injustice, but nowhere do you find him throwing himself into the arena to do battle with the oppressor, or devoting his efforts to help his neighbor. The preacher is a sad and lonely man, without friends, who evaluates his world solely in terms of himself.

I remember hearing a legend about a man who had a poisoned arrow sticking in his flesh. Instead of pulling it out, the man studies the arrow with long and deliberate concentration. He muses to himself, "I wonder of what kind of wood this shaft is made? From what bird do these feathers come? And the person who loosed this bolt — was he short or tall, dark or fair?"

Finally, those who are standing close by can no longer endure this mental exercise and they cry, "Pull the arrow out! It is poisoned! Pull the arrow out before you die!"

The Preacher is like that man. He has been pierced by evil and suffering in this world. But he does not contend with it. All he does is study the size, shape, and quality of the arrow, and it eventually poisons him with the venom of despair.

I have been hard on the Preacher, but I am still glad we have his words in our Bible. To the Preacher belongs the credit for setting forth, with compelling realism, the problem of existence. He is to be praised for his candor in evaluating the dark side of the human condition. The subject of his writing — life, and how best to appraise and use it — lies at the heart of all religions.

The Christian faith does not dodge the issues raised by Ecclesiastes. It measures those issues against the stature of Jesus Christ. Even though Christ knew the worst that was in all people, he also knew the best, and he believed in the power of God to bring it to pass. What promises Christ makes to us! "Greater works than mine shall you do." What claims he lays upon us! "You are the light of the world and the salt of the earth." How huge is his trust in us! "You are all my friends; love one another as I have loved you." How valuable he considers each person! "The Father knows your needs before you ask him."

The Preacher did not know Jesus Christ. But he did know the God of Abraham, Isaac, Jacob, and Joseph. He did know the God of the prophets. Yet he still chose not to believe that there was a redemptive factor in creation, even though he might acknowledge the need for one. It is a solemn and terrible thing to be a free soul. Each one of us chooses the god in whom we will believe and through whom we will live.

Ecclesiastes represents the bankruptcy of human thinking and the barrenness of egoism. To have this book in the Bible does, however, throw a light upon our need for reconciliation with God and with each other. In fact, these words of despair may be one of the most startling predictions of the coming of Christ. God sent his Son of gladness into the world to demonstrate to the sons of sadness that the Preacher and those who follow him have not seen everything under the sun. The world is not merely a cruel joke, but rather the cradle of the Father's love for all the children of his creation.

Proverbs
In Quest of the Good Life

Proverbs 1:1-7, 20-23; 2:1-10

For three weeks, we are exploring together the Wisdom books of the Old Testament: Ecclesiastes, Proverbs, and Job. This literature is the product of an influential group of sages who flourished in Israel from the fourth to the first century B.C. They provided a complement and a corrective to the prophets and the priests of Israel, and they were responsible for popularizing religion for the common folk of the nation. They spoke to their questions: "Does life have a meaning? How can I get along day by day? Why does an innocent person suffer?"

Last week, we dealt with the gloomy book of Ecclesiastes, written by a man who called himself the Preacher. And what a strange preacher he is, for his sermons about life carry a message of skepticism and despair. He speaks the truth, and we can applaud him for his candor and powers of observation, but he has no sense of the unseen and finds no profit in sacrifice and love. His message is that life is a vapor and there is nothing new under the sun. In his application of wisdom, the writer of Ecclesiastes fashions a literary product of unbearable pessimism.

Now, Proverbs is a different matter. It contains the distilled wisdom of more than six centuries of Hebrew thought and experience. Unlike Ecclesiastes, it sounds the note of optimism and the good life. To be sure, many of the authors who contribute to this book share the same world view as Ecclesiastes; namely, that there is no eternal significance to life, but they do not find it necessary to dwell upon such morbid speculation. They are too busy talking to people, going out to dinner, or walking through the marketplace picking up the lustrous gems of beauty, humor and truth, to spend time complaining.

I have often wondered if the Preacher in Ecclesiastes was a neglected child, for he makes no mention of the solidarity and support of family life which has always been characteristic of the religion of Israel. This is not the case with Proverbs. Large portions of this book are cast in a paternal framework. We hear the father of the family patiently instructing his son about the pitfalls and possibilities of life. He teaches him how to make his way through it with the least number of wounds, and the greatest portion of fulfillment and satisfaction.

Chapter after chapter begins with such phrases as, "My sons, if you receive my teaching . . ."; "Hear, O sons, a father's instruction . . ."; "My son, be attentive to my words . . ." The writers of Proverbs would approve, I am sure, of such admonitions in our day as, "The family that prays together stays together," or "Go to church this week as a family."

I suspect that writings such as Proverbs were more popular than we might imagine during the closing years of the pre-Christian era. Prophecy was in decline. The law was calcified. The reconstruction period after the exile was over. These wise men must have traveled the country roads and glided through the city streets, speaking with an international, eloquent, and practical flair that was exciting and fresh compared to the mystical visions of the prophets and the stylized incantations of the priests. Like the prophets, they went out to the people. But instead of shouting, "Thus says the Lord!", they spoke smoothly about how to be moral and upright in day to day living.

Proverbs speaks approvingly of an honest day's labor:

A slack hand causes poverty, but the hand of the diligent makes rich. (Proverbs 10:4)

It counsels against gossip and slander:

He who belittles his neighbor lacks sense, but a man of understanding remains silent. (Proverbs 11:12)

It encourages honest business dealings:

A false balance is an abomination to the Lord, but a just weight is his delight. (Proverbs 11:1)

It advises young women in the arts of propriety:

Like a gold ring in a swine's snout, is a beautiful woman without discretion. (Proverbs 11:22)

And it assists young couples as they think about marriage to pursue love and trust rather than money:

Better is a little with the fear of the Lord than great treasure and trouble with it. Better is a dinner of herbs where love is than a fatted ox and hatred with it. (Proverbs 15:16-17)

Because the wise men knew that brevity was the soul of wit, and that people were more concerned with how to get along in life than how to get to heaven, they commanded the attention of the troubled and the young. They knew how to win friends and influence people, and there may even be some evidence that, for a fee, they would tell you how to do the same thing, too.

Behind some of the majestic thought of Second Isaiah there may be a condemnation of the sages for their witty words, their easy answers, and their money-making motives. One wonders if Isaiah's nose is out of joint when he writes:

Ho, everyone who thirsts, come to the waters; and he who has no money, come, buy and eat! Come, buy wine and milk without money and *without price. Why do you spend your money for that which is not bread, and your labor for that which does not satisfy? Harken diligently to me, and eat what is good, and delight yourself in fatness. (Isaiah 55:1-2)*

It is a fact that the sages of Israel were spiritual middlemen who mediated the exalted doctrines of the prophets and interpreted them in terms of common life and experience. In some respects they did succeed where the prophets failed. Our Judeo-Christian tradition regards the prophets as the most incisive exponents of the Old Testament spirit. Yet, one cannot help wondering if these spiritual experts would have been so permanent and far-reaching without the work of the wise men who made popular, to some extent, the prophetic ideals.

With the solvent of sympathy they came close to people's needs and perhaps, just a bit, plowed the ground into which the seed of Jesus Christ would later fall, causing the New Testament evangelists to say that the common people heard him gladly.

While it is true that the wise men do not deal with Israel's hope of a Messiah, neither do they confine themselves to the narrow nationalism so often exhibited by Old Testament Judaism. They are interested in people as people. They would applaud the apostle Paul when he says:

There is neither Jew nor Greek, there is neither slave nor free, there is neither male nor female; for you are all one in Christ Jesus. (Galatians 3:28)

The sages of Israel would look with great joy, not so much upon our exalted councils and commissions, and high level talks in government, the United Nations, or in the church, but rather upon those agencies and movements where people join together to meet each other's needs, improve living conditions, and understand each other. They would like the Peace Corps, Unicef, Vista, and all those local citizen organizations that address community issues.

Finally, those who stand behind the wisdom in the book of Proverbs have given us a legacy in the word "wisdom." It is an inheritance upon which the New Testament builds. In general, the ancient Hebrew's main interest was in right conduct. He cared about the way you walked, rather than how much you talked. Wisdom dealt with the way you walked.

Proverbs defines religion as wisdom. Wisdom is the fundamental principle in the universe. To live by wisdom's precepts is to be in harmony with the Creator. This is so important in Proverbs, that wisdom takes on human proportions. Thus we read:

> Wisdom cries aloud in the street; in the markets she raises her voice; on the top of the walls she cries out; at the entrance of the city gates she speaks . . . (Proverbs 1:20-21)

The New Testament writers used this idea of wisdom, upon which many of them were weaned themselves, as a means to present Jesus Christ to a pagan world that glorified the wise debater and the skillful thinker as the norm of the good, pious, and successful life. The authors of Proverbs did much to develop the idea of wisdom, but they touched too lightly and too simply upon the eternal questions of human existence. They solved the inequities of life too easily. Sin and suffering were a matter of black and white, cause and consequence. If you were good and just, you would prosper. If not, you would suffer poverty and pain. Proverbs does not take into account the gray shades of life.

It took a Job to challenge the god of the wise men by asking the question of why he, who was innocent of wrong-doing, should suffer. It took some of the Psalmists to doubt the easy answers of punishment and reward. It took a Second Isaiah to sing a song of a servant who suffered for others;

But he was wounded for our transgressions, he was bruised for our iniquities; upon him was the chastisement that made us whole, and with his stripes we are healed . . . and the Lord has laid on him the iniquity of us all. (Isaiah 53:5-6)

Our Christian faith encourages us to love the Lord our God with all our minds. But it also insists that we cannot save ourselves through our own wisdom. The tug of the total religious experience of the Hebrew people held in check the making of wisdom into a god. The Greeks and the Romans had no such religious memory. They did venerate wisdom and reason. Paul's great appeal to the philosophers and wise men in Athens (Acts 17:16-34) was a failure because he talked about a God who acted in a most unwise way. The God of Paul revealed himself through a man who foolishly became a man for others, instead of a teacher who would show you how to get along with equanimity in life. All this man got for his trouble was death, and the wise man never played that card until he had no other choice.

The Greeks in Athens welcomed debate on how God loves his world through nature, order, and reason. But they could not accept the death and resurrection of a carpenter as the supreme demonstration of that love.

And even Israel, which was beginning to chafe under the wise man's plea for moderation, was disappointed in Jesus Christ. Rather than lead them to war, he wanted to lead them to God and to their neighbor, and that neighbor might well be a Roman or a Samaritan. A messiah who allowed himself to be crucified was an unspeakable offense.

In many respects, these same dissatisfactions with the way of Christ are still with us. He does not condone what we do, even though we have more sophisticated ways of trampling upon each other, and more subtle means of transgressing the commandments. The crucified and risen Christ is still a stumbling-block for those who put all their eggs in the wisdom basket of the world.

But the God of Jesus Christ was wise also. By choosing foolishness; by choosing the weak and despised; by choosing love and forgiveness, suffering, and death as vehicles for meaning, he gave our questions about life eternal significance. He answered them with a Word made flesh.

The wisdom of Proverbs does win an affectionate place in our hearts. It offers much for the worthy living of our days. But for the meaning of our days — for answers to the questions that bombard us such as, "Am I known, or am I alone?" "Am I born to give, or am I born to get?" "Am I loved, or am I lost?" — Jesus Christ is the only one who answers those queries to our satisfaction and for our salvation.

Wretched man that I am! Who will deliver me from this body of death? Thanks be to God through Jesus Christ our Lord! (Romans 7:24-25)

Job
Written With a Pen
Dipped in Tears

Job 17 and 21; Matthew 27:45-50

Today, we conclude our examination of the wisdom literature in the Old Testament. The three primary spokesmen for the wisdom school are Ecclesiastes, Proverbs, and Job. These three filled a vacuum that developed in Israel from the fourth to the first century B.C. The prophets had fallen into disrepute, and the priests were more enamored of law than of life. Only the wise men kept in contact with the common people, speaking to hard questions in a popular way. What they said was not always hopeful, but it was helpful in keeping alive the burning concerns all persons have.

For example, Ecclesiastes is not a confident book to read. Its thesis is that life has no ultimate meaning. But given the "misery loves company" feeling that afflicts all of us from time to time, the reader often derives a strange warmth from this book's cold conclusion.

Proverbs, on the other hand, is a bouncy, witty, practical book about living the good life. It does not dwell on the morbid, nor does it deal with the mysteries of God and eternity. It is written for the moment and expounds the wisdom of moral and ethical conduct in human relationships.

But today, we come to Job, and we are faced with another cut of cloth from the fabric of life. Here is a book that almost defies sermonic comment. Job must be felt. It is written with a pen dipped in tears. Its words are fashioned in the soul rather than the mind. Job throws down the gauntlet before the question, "Why does a good and innocent person suffer?"

Between Job's confrontation in his own flesh with that question, and the conclusion he reaches, we witness the awful pilgrimage of a human soul between heaven and hell — between faith and black despair — hammering out upon the anvil of existence a belief that there *is* meaning to his misery. Job does not give us the answers we might like to have, such as avoidance. What he does is nerve us with the message that a human being can go through torment and come out of it being more than when he entered the dark night of the soul.

What I would like to do this morning is put the book in context for you, suggest the ebb and flow of its movement, and encourage you to consider Jesus Christ as the conclusion to this poem of agony. After all, he is the yardstick by which we measure all the experiences of life. And then, finally, I should like to comment upon how this minister tries to respond to the cry of the sufferer he meets, both in himself, and in this parish.

So then, what about the book itself? Job should be divided into two parts, the prose section and the poetic section. The prose narrative consists of the first two chapters and the last ten verses of the book. It is most likely an ancient tale written and resurrected to support the then-current belief that the righteous prosper and the sinner suffers punishment.

Now, after all, even those who subscribed to this simplistic explanation for suffering saw many contradictions to it in their own experience. So the prose narrative stands as a confirmation that, even though a truly righteous man might suffer, like Job, it is really God testing the authentic nature of a person's goodness by submerging him beneath the waters of torment. If he proves true, his fortunes will be restored to him four-fold. So then, this first part of the book stands as an archetype of suffering for the old, naive theology and was possibly used to buttress up the system in the face of devastating contradictions.

Job, however, becomes immortal when an unknown author takes this narrative and uses it as a springboard to call the old theology a lie! The large poetic portion of the book of Job is a protest and a challenge against the current doctrine that sin and suffering always go together. The author wants to show that there is a mystery in suffering which cannot be completely understood — a mystery that goes back to God and results in the fact that some who are innocent and righteous do suffer, just as some who are guilty and intransigent prosper and are at ease.

So, as we read the book of Job, we are hearing a man tell, in naked self-revelation, the story of a spiritual agony. It is spiritual rather than physical because, as he suffers, Job never challenges the existence of God. Instead, his battle is fought around God's nature. Is God at heart good, or is he evil? Is he faithful, or capricious? It has been said it is easier to suffer if you do not believe in God, for all you need do is endure the torment itself. It is the divine prefix which adds the additional dimension of agony and calls forth the question, "My God, my God, why have you forsaken me?"

More than once Job comes close to renouncing God in order to preserve his sanity. But there break in upon him the moments of blessing in the past that he took for granted then, but which sustain him now. On one occasion, Job appeals to the infinite pains God took to weave together the human body of the unborn child:

Thy hands fashioned and made me; and now
thou dost turn about and destroy me.

Remember that thou hast made me of clay; and wilt thou turn me to dust again?

Thou didst clothe me with skin and flesh, and knit me together with bones and sinews. Thou hast granted me life and steadfast love; and thy care has preserved my spirit. Yet these things thou didst hide in thy heart; I know that this was thy purpose. (Job 10:8-9; 11-13)

Perhaps Alfred Tennyson had those words in mind when he wrote in his "In Memoriam":

Thou wilt not leave us in the dust:
Thou madest man, he knows not why,
He thinks he was not made to die;
And thou hast made him: thou art just.

The author of Job did not have a concept of eternal life such as that in which Christians believe. We must understand that his plea is not for that. His cry is for the knowledge of why the days of the righteous are dislocated before their time — why sorrow, sickness, and death are insinuated into life before it has been lived to the fulness of years.

The old theology of suffering-equals-sin even makes itself felt in the quality of friendship. The book of Job carefully draws a picture of three friends who come to comfort him in his grief. Their well-meant words of solace disintegrate into debate and stimulate Job to some of his wildest outbreaks.

Eliphaz, Bildad, and Zophar, the three friends, each has his own personal approach to Job's problem. Eliphaz speaks with a gentle mysticism; Bildad is a dry traditionalist; and Zophar is dogmatic and narrowminded. Yet, all three operate from one unswerving position: God must punish evil and reward good. All evildoers are sufferers. Job is a sufferer. Therefore, Job is an evildoer. With that conclusion, friendship is poisoned and, while they may not say so, Job becomes, for them, unclean.

And finally, God is not silent in this book. His response to Job often seems so irrelevant that you wonder why Job continues to believe in a deity who prattles on about the heavens, the sea, the light, the wind, the hippo, and the crocodile. "God, all I want to know is why you are doing this to me, and all you talk about is everything except me!"

God's cosmic sermons, however, seem to be illustrations of his wisdom and power which he applies to human ignorance and weakness. The sermons are designed to teach Job humility. And Job does admit that there may be a wise, but hidden, purpose to his suffering.

Well, that is about as far as we are led toward an answer of why the innocent and righteous suffer. There might be a further clue in the council of heaven in the prologue where we see God allowing Satan to test Job. It is, after all, God who calls attention to Job. It is God who permits the test of his faith, who watches the experiment and sets the limits. The tone is that the will of God is being done, witness God's first words in the book: "Have you considered my servant, Job?" It is possible the book is saying God trusts his faithful people to stand by his truth, even in extreme adversity, and that one can hold on to God in faith, not for what he gives, but just for himself. Whichever way we interpret Job's suffering, he was a gladiator for God, a spectacle to heaven and to earth.

And Jesus Christ — was he also a gladiator for God, a spectacle to heaven and to earth? Yes, we often speak of him that way. How does Paul say it?

For our sake he (God) made him to be sin who knew no sin, so that in him we might become the righteousness of God. (2 Corinthians 5:21)

While the book of Job does not completely satisfy our minds regarding the question of suffering, it does begin to go beneath the surface of our human explanations and plumb the depths of the mind of God. Job does insist that when the innocent suffer, they cannot be indicted for their wickedness. Job does suggest that some suffering can have behind it a divine purpose. And Job does illustrate that a person can move through much suffering and maintain, yes, even strengthen his or her faith by remembering the acts of God which were acknowledged in some brighter, fairer day.

As a Christian minister I often find I have a dual role with those who suffer. I am represented by my office and by my person. With those I do not know very well, my office as minister is much more important for their moment of darkness than my person which is unfamiliar. They see in my vocational identity someone whose task it is to give pain meaning and thereby make it bearable. And, of course, I make my appeal to the promises of the gospel that there are worlds beyond our present understanding, that the loving God does not vindictively intend us to suffer, and that Jesus Christ is the illustration of much that is a mystery to us.

But with those I know intimately, both as pastor and as friend, the suffering experience becomes, at one and the same time, both more deeply meaningful and more acute. In a situation like this, whatever comfort and release is managed between us is not only the result of our sharing the gospel promises, but also due to the knowledge of each other as mutual sufferers who stand under the same judgment and the same joy. At a time like this it is my person that gives credibility to my office.

This is why it is so important for the fellowship of the church to be a mutual ministry of intimate sharing and patience, of crying together and laughing together. This must be the burden of all of us, not just the professional staff. We know, along with Job, that intellect is not enough to work our way through pain. The white-hot flame of suffering is not conducive to mental gymnastics. We stand utterly alone in the middle of it and it threatens to consume us. While no one else can totally share its intensity, how important it is to know that there are those who stand close enough to us to be warmed by that flame and confirm that we are not abandoned.

In his suffering experience Job did not witness another person sharing his pain with him. His three friends grieved only over the fact that they were betrayed in their assessment of Job. Our faith asks us to be friends of Christ rather than friends of Job when we stand with another in their darkness. It may be that the only way they will catch a vision of their God when their eyes are glazed with pain and tears is through our presence. God does speak through the senses. His presence is communicated through our touch, our words, and even our silence. Yes, it hurts to be confronted with another's pain, but that is one of the labors of love that God lays upon his people.

Sometimes we worry so much about our faith, our belief and our trust, that we forget Christ came not only to make us good but to make us faithful. Just as important is God's faith and belief and trust in *us*. He calls us, not just to be saved, but to serve. And it may be that in our serving, our helping, and our healing the answer to suffering lies there.

Prayer in Affliction

Keep me from bitterness. It is so easy
To nurse sharp, bitter thoughts each dull
    dark hour.
Against self-pity, Man of sorrows, defend me,
With Thy deep sweetness and Thy gentle
    power.

*And out of all this hurt of pain and
heartbreak
Help me to harvest a new sympathy
For suffering human kind, a wiser pity
For those who lift a heavier cross with Thee.* *

Violet Alleyn Storey

---

*James Dalton Morrison, ed., *Masterpieces of Religious Verse*, (New York: Harper and Row.)

III.

The

Gospels

The Gospel of Mark
Written to Help Us Run

Mark 10:35-45

This month we are going to examine the four Gospels in our New Testament — Mark, Matthew, Luke, and John. They are our primary record of Jesus of Nazareth whose life and ministry caused the other books of the New Testament to be written, and which help us make sense out of a large part of the Old Testament.

The Gospels were written by four men who were seized, like us, by the life of Jesus. They were led to leave a record of his life and work as they saw it. Each writer sees Jesus differently. Each is attracted to a part of his personality and tries to make that part come through clearly in his record.

Also, each writer has a need which Jesus meets for him. And each writer reflects the fulfillment of that need through the emphasis of his book. But all the Gospel writers agree on one main point: God used human flesh to act decisively in the world by showing the world what he is like and what his intentions are for his creation. In Jesus, God says, "I treasure you so much — love you so deeply — that I will show you what true life really is like. I will come to you, live with you, and even die for you!"

I begin with the Gospel of Mark today because it was written first, even though it does not appear first in the Bible. Matthew and Luke, and to some small extent, John, all copy from Mark with the exception of about thirty verses. Mark is the foundation upon which the others build. So, let's look at the Gospel of

Mark, a book written to help us run.

Run? How? Where? And who wants to run, anyway? We're out of breath from running all week. We've come to church to slow down. What kind of running is asked of us in the gospel of Mark? The sermon title was chosen to catch up the feeling you get as you read Mark. Mark takes seriously the words in Habakkuk 2:2-3:

Write the vision; make it plain upon tablets, so he may run who reads it. For still the vision awaits its time; it hastens to the end — it will not lie.

You can't saunter through the book of Mark. You jog and trot, and sometimes dash for your life to keep up with the Master. I think the movement in this Gospel says something about what the author, Mark, discovers in the personality of Jesus that meets his deepest needs.

The pace of the book makes you wonder what Mark was like; what made him write an account of Jesus that stands apart in its briefness, its clarity, and its urgent character. Mark uses an economy of words. He prefers verbs to adjectives — .action in favor of description. You don't mistake his meanings. He wants you to get the message the first time, so he can move on to the next point. Thus, he writes like this:

And he began to teach them that the Son of man must suffer many things, and be rejected by the elders and the chief priests and the scribes, and be killed, and after three days rise again. And he said this plainly. (Mark 8:31-32)

All we know about Mark is that he was sometimes called John, that his mother's name was Mary, and that it was in his house in Jerusalem that the church gathered in its earliest days. Possibly the last supper was eaten in Mark's house, conceivably making him the only Gospel writer who was an eyewitness to the last days of Jesus' ministry.

We know that this John Mark was an interpreter for Peter and traveled with him, even to Rome, surely learning more about Jesus from him. Some of the writings of the church Fathers during the first two centuries speak of John Mark as the author of this book.

What kind of man was Mark? I imagine he was fiery and impatient, chafing under the organizational agonies of the young church, and not very cordial to the inter-office feud between Peter and Paul. I think Mark was torn apart by the cruelty and injustice of his time, and by the political intrigue that went on in Jerusalem as men jockeyed for power and curried the favor of Rome to line their pockets.

Mark would be a front-line worker in our cities today, or an advocate for migrant workers or the American Indian, trying to secure basic rights for neglected people. He would be a champion of job-training for minority groups, the right to work, decent housing, and adequate food for all people. We can only guess at these things about Mark from the way he writes about Jesus, painting a picture of God's man with a mission — God's man on the move. For Mark, Jesus gets down to business in revolutionary rather than evolutionary terms.

In forty-five verses Mark accomplishes what it takes Luke five chapters to do. In forty-five verses Jesus is born, baptized, tempted, chooses his team, teaches in several synagogues, heals a madman, Peter's mother-in-law, and a leper, and is famous throughout the entire region of Galilee.

Mark's favorite word is "immediately." "Immediately he saw the heavens opened" . . . "The Spirit immediately drove him out into the wilderness." "And immediately they left their nets and followed him." "And immediately he called them."

"Immediately on the sabbath he entered the synagogue and taught." "And immediately he left the synagogue . . ." "Immediately the leprosy left him . . ."

Mark's Jesus leads his disciples on breathlessly, with little time to reflect upon what has happened. Jesus is moving to a rendezvous when all things will become clear. "Just stick with me until then, and you'll understand," he seems to say. They stick with him as he rushes up and down the land until, finally, Jesus stops by the side of the dusty road, waits while his disciples catch up to him, and then tells who he is, why he has come, and where he is going.

This focal point in the Gospel of Mark is our text. He tells his disciples that his ministry in Galilee is finished. He has healed; he has taught; great crowds have come to him. He has met the needs of many neglected people. Now, a confrontation is coming with the leaders of the nation. The power of God must meet head-on the power of vested interest. He says to his friends:

> You know that those who are supposed to rule over the Gentiles lord it over them, and their great men exercise authority over them. But it shall not be so among you; but whoever would be great among you must be your servant, and whoever would be first among you must be slave of all. For the Son of man also came not to be served but to serve, and to give his life as a ransom for many. (Mark 10:42-45)

Two kinds of power must do battle with each other if people are to be helped. The power of love for people must clash with the power of love for things. Mark goes on from this point using the last third of his book to tell about the last seven days of Jesus' ministry. In this last portion, his Jesus illustrates true greatness, which is not only to live for others, but also a willingness to die for them so all persons can inherit the kingdom which was God's intention from the beginning.

Mark, the social reformer — Mark, the champion of justice, saw in Jesus not only one who taught, healed, served, and battled against evil, but also one who taught those who followed him to do the same. In Jesus' mind, every human being was a child of God and a neighbor to others, if not in fact, at least ideally. If he could get people to live out all that it meant to call God, Father, and call another human being, neighbor, then he would make out of every person what God intended him to be.

The only way this could happen was through love, not in a sentimental sense, but in a hard, social sense of unselfishness, mercy, justice, and single-hearted devotion to the good of another. In a love like this a lower self is lost and a higher self is found.

Mark felt an urgency for this kind of love. A profligate and brutal empire made him write with haste and fashion a picture of Jesus as one who had no time to waste. Mark's man of action is still valid for us today, for we have no time to waste. Mark writes plainly and with a bite to his words so that we who read may run, not away from responsibility, not chasing rainbows, nor aimlessly in circles, but run to meet the cries of pain, anger, grief, loneliness, and hunger which inhabit the shadows everywhere.

Mark writes to help us run after the true greatness of Jesus. It is a greatness of serving which he says we, too, can exhibit. The disciples discovered that Christ was always up ahead of them blazing trails, laying foundations, and unearthing opportunities for them to build on and complete. Mark wants us to discover the same thing.

The book of Hebrews catches and completes the spirit which Mark conveys in his gospel. Take these words with you and make them your own:

Therefore, since we are surrounded by so great a cloud of witnesses, let us lay aside every weight, and sin which clings so closely, and let us run with perseverance the race that is set before us, looking to Jesus the pioneer and perfecter of our faith, who for the joy that was set before him endured the cross, despising the shame, and is seated at the right hand of the throne of God.

Consider him who endured from sinners such hostility against himself, so that you may not grow weary or faint-hearted. (Hebrews 12:1-3)

The Gospel of Matthew
A Teacher Sent From God

Matthew 5:17-20

This month we are looking at the four Gospels as total books. Our purpose for this overview is to stimulate us to read again the accounts of the life of Jesus Christ. Each Gospel writer had his own needs which he laid before Christ, just as we do. They, too, searched for meaning to their days, and for answers to the enigmas that faced them as religious individuals and as citizens of a nation.

In Jesus, each Gospel writer found his deepest need satisfied, had his thorniest question answered, his worst fear calmed, his greatest joy confirmed. The natural thing to do when writing about Jesus is to focus upon that need he has met in your life. This is precisely what Mark, Matthew, Luke, and John do. These are Gospels as they see him.

How fortunate we are they wrote this way, for taken all together, the Gospels show us the mind and the method of the Master in a way that no one person could accomplish. And since Jesus is greater than all his commentators, there are still Gospels to be written, according to each of us.

But even you and I must have basic material to work with. That is why we explore these first records of our faith. I began with Mark last week. Even though he does not appear first in the New Testament, he is the first to record the mighty acts of God in Jesus Christ. Mark is basic. He lays the foundations upon which the other writers build.

In Mark's mind, Jesus was a man of action, turning

the world upside down in a clash of powers — the power of God and the power of the world. Mark's Gospel is urgent. In it, the disenfranchised of earth cry out for a champion, a savior, and they are not disappointed, just as Mark was not disappointed. Jesus meets Mark's need for one who "came not to be served but to serve, and give his life as a ransom for many."

But now as we enter the Gospel of Matthew, we encounter a change of climate from that found in Mark. We shift from the electric to the educational; from the street-corner tract which is meant to inflame, to the textbook which is meant to instruct. When you move from Mark to Matthew you slow down from a run to a walk and, in many places, you simply sit down and listen to the master teacher sent from God. This is Matthew's emphasis; the teacher sent from God. And this is Matthew's need, to find one whose teaching has eternal integrity, and who answers the deepest questions of thinkers in every age.

We have very little information about who Matthew was, or what he was like, but I think his Gospel gives us some substantial clues. These clues are summed up in an anonymous rhyme quoted by Archibald M. Hunter in his book, *Introducing the New Testament*. It goes like this:

Matthew gives us five discourses;
In threes and sevens he likes his sources;
He writes to show what O.T. meant,
With an ecclesiastic bent.

Let's look at each phrase of this rhyme, for it catches up the special features of Matthew's book.

1. First, "Matthew gives us five discourses." Matthew's Gospel is divided into five parts with an introduction about the birth of Jesus, and an epilogue on his death and resurrection. These five parts, or discourses, are really systematic groupings of Jesus'

teachings. The first part, the Sermon on the Mount, is most familiar to us. But the others are just as important for understanding Jesus' mind and Matthew's purpose. They are the charge to the twelve disciples, the parables about the kingdom of heaven, a section on true greatness and forgiveness, and finally, a discourse on the last judgment.

As Jesus journeys from birth to death and resurrection, Matthew has him stop five times and teach his followers why he walks this way. For the Jew, the five books of Moses were designed to do the same thing. Thus Matthew, the learned Jew, with the aroma of the law still clinging to him, presents the five books of Christ, not to cancel out, but to complete the journey his people began so long ago.

2. The second line of the rhyme reads, "In threes and sevens he likes his sources." In Matthew you encounter these two numbers over and over again. The book begins with three groups of names. An angel speaks three times to Joseph. Peter denies his Lord three times. Pilate asks Jesus three questions. There are three miracles, seven parables, and seven woes.

This tendency to number grouping is not superstitious. It is systematic and reflects the organizational mind of a teacher who was accustomed to providing his students with memory aids. Matthew, the Jewish teacher, wants us to remember what he discovered as the most important thing in his life. The use of numerical device is not beneath his dignity.

You might try this exercise sometime. Write down all the quotes you can remember from the Gospels. Don't worry if they are exactly right or not. It is likely that most of them come from Matthew. He writes to help us remember.

3. The rhyme continues, "He writes to show what O.T. meant." Now this is Matthew's focus. This is what

the text said. "Think not that I have come to abolish the law and the prophets; I have come not to abolish them but to fulfill them." Matthew, the Jewish teacher of religious law, found that Jesus filled the aching void which the Old Testament commandments, ordinances, and interpretations could not. Under the law a person could live and prosper, pray and serve, reasonably well. But the law did not conquer sin. The law did not leap over national boundaries. The law still left the people in an interrogative mood; "My God, where are you? Why must you always be the one who is 'to come,' rather than the one who is 'with us'?"

Jesus changed all that for Matthew, so that his entire Gospel shouts, "Jesus is the Christ, the Son of God! He came not to destroy the law of Moses, but to fulfill it and teach us a more excellent way of life as members of a new community, the church — a new and holy nation, destined to embrace all the world!"

In Matthew's Gospel we find more Old Testament quotations than in all the others. He demonstrates how Jesus completes the old covenant. Eight times he calls him the son of David. He has Peter call him the Messiah. No more waiting, no more hoping, no more discouragement looking for him who is to come. Fellow Jews, he has come! Now you can begin to live the new life God has promised for all people! The master rabbi of all — the teacher of teachers — has been sent from God to show us a more excellent way, and all must sit at his feet and listen.

4. So then, we come to the end of the rhyme, "With an ecclesiastic bent." Matthew writes for the young church. He is the only Gospel writer who uses the word "church." His book is a catechism for new Christians. It acquaints them with the church, not as a building, or a budget, or a business with bold schemes for attracting new members, but as a household of power gathered around its teacher who is the source

of that power, and to whom they must return continually to renew their strength.

Matthew has a preoccupation with the words, "kingdom of heaven." He sees the church as a little corner of that kingdom, already existing in time with its fulness yet to come. The teacher sent from God remains in spirit with this little corner of the kingdom and teaches the church about itself so that it can go out into the world confidently knowing that it speaks for him.

††††

So, Matthew, the teacher, shows us another side of Christ as teacher. Sometimes his passion for using prophecy to prove the importance of Christ may leave us a bit skeptical. Yet, behind his "crystal ball" technique is the thesis that Christianity is not an accident. It is a fulfillment of God's saving purposes begun in the history of a tiny land at the end of the Mediterranean Sea. The people of this land were used by God to speak to every human being on the planet about what it means to love, to forgive and be forgiven, and to be servants.

It is no accident that Matthew is the first book in the New Testament. His words end the question-mark mood of the Old Testament and declare in the imperative mood, "His name shall be called 'God with us.' " And Matthew's last words lead you into the future, "Lo, I am with you always, even to the end of the age!"

Matthew invites us to be led into the heart and mind of the teacher sent from God. He invites us to discover that the aim of this teacher is not only to inform us, but also to change us and send us out into the world shouting, "World, world, listen! It is not the beginning of the end. It is the end of the beginning, and the best is yet to be!"

The Gospel of Luke
Healing the Wounds
of the World

Jeremiah 8:18-22
Luke 4:16-21

The four Gospels, Matthew, Mark, Luke, and John are our sermon themes for this month. They represent the major record of Jesus Christ's ministry. They are the center around which the church gathers for strength, comfort, and direction. In the broadest sense, the Gospels are biographical writing. However, they differ from other biographies because they are written not only to inform us, but primarily to change us.

Now, in the Gospels there are two biographies. Standing in the shadows behind the Master is the man who writes about him. The Gospels not only tell us about the mind of Christ, but also about the mind of the evangelist who shows him to us. This is the way we are looking at the Gospels this month — from the point of view of why the author emphasizes what he does about Jesus in his story. You see, the reason Jesus meets our needs through the record we have is because he first met the deep needs of those who wrote about him.

We looked at Mark first because it was written first. Mark pictures Jesus on an urgent mission — a man of action striding boldly through the world with his disciples running breathlessly behind to keep up. Mark's Jesus wastes no time confronting injustice in the world and upsetting the distorted value systems of people. We concluded that Mark himself agonized over the inequities of life and found in Christ one who met them head-on.

Matthew shows us a different side of Jesus. He reveals him as a teacher sent from God. Matthew divides his Gospel into five teaching sections written to the young church to strengthen it against opposition. Also, Matthew writes to the Jewish community saying, "Your waiting is over. The law has been fulfilled. The teacher sent from God brought the powers of love to bear upon the misplaced priorities of the world and was victorious. He is the one who is to come!"

Matthew, the Jewish teacher of religious law, sat at the feet of a greater teacher and wrote a new course of study for the hungry human spirit.

Today, we come to the Gospel of Luke. This is my favorite life of Christ. In its form and content there is nothing more beautiful than Luke's story. The language is superb and its beauty has survived translation.

Luke's message embraces the whole world. Christ becomes the man of every time. While Matthew is often called the Jewish gospel, Luke is called the Gentile gospel. But it is even more than that. It is a universal gospel. As you read, you get the feeling that this Christ of Luke's reaches out his arms and embraces our spinning planet, drawing it to his breast. The Christ we meet in Luke comes to heal the gaping wounds of the world, found not only in Israel, but wherever people are lonely, poor, sick, and crushed by guilt.

What need does Jesus meet in Luke's life that makes him write in such a compassionate and universal way? We get our answer when we find out who Luke was. There is quite a bit of information available to us.

From the way he writes, and the magnificent use he makes of the Greek language, we know he was not a Jew. He was a Greek, and a very well educated one at that, for a small portion of his book is written in the highly refined language of the philosopher, man of science, and man of letters.

We also know that Luke wrote a portion of the book of Acts as an early history of the young church. His introductions in both books are highly refined and addressed to a Roman official in a high position. In the opening words of Acts, he says that his first book (the Gospel) dealt with all that Jesus did and taught, and now the second book will deal with the results of his teaching.

We know that Luke traveled with Paul on his missionary journeys and that Paul calls him "the beloved physician." (Colossians 4:14) Luke was a Greek physician, widely traveled and skilled in the healing of his day. Even his writing betrays his profession. Doctor Luke is forever giving medical opinions and prescribing treatments.

In the account of the healing of Peter's mother-in-law, which Luke borrowed from Mark, Mark merely comments in passing that she had a fever. But Luke insists on telling us she had a high fever.

In the parable of the good Samaritan, doctor Luke demonstrates how you should care for a person who has been badly beaten. You pour on oil and wine to cleanse the injured area, and then you bind up the wound to keep out foreign matter. Then you take the patient to an inn where better treatment can be given, and you tell the proprietor you will be back in a day or two to see how the patient is coming along.

One of the most interesting clues to Luke's profession appears in that well-known saying of Jesus, "For it is easier for a camel to go through the eye of a needle than for a rich man to enter the kingdom of God." (Luke 18:25) Mark and Matthew include the same verse in their Gospels. But while they use the word for a sewing needle, Luke inserts the word for a surgical needle.

I wonder what it was like to be a physician in the ancient world. How discouraging it must have been to dedicate your life to healing and wholeness, and still be surrounded on every side by disease, disability, and death. If I were Luke, I would rage against the universe at the thought that there was not enough knowledge and resource to successfully deal with all the human wreckage that came for help. I imagine his percentage of success was quite low.

Also, Luke certainly knew from observation that the body was not the only part of a person subject to sickness. The mind and the soul also crumbled under hate, guilt, loneliness, and lack of self-respect.

And finally, learned man that he was, doctor Luke knew well that the philosophies and the superstitious, mystery religions of his time offered no balm in Gilead to heal the sin-sick soul.

Luke needed to find someone, somewhere, who could win the ba...e against death, the premature death of the body, and the living death of the withered or broken spirit. In Jesus Christ he found both a teacher and a colleague. Jesus, the master physician, had the skill to cut deep and clean out the infections that maim people.

One way to discover the spiritual commitment of a person is to look for those things that make him angry. The things that made Luke angry are seen in the emphases he places upon Jesus' ministry.

Luke's Jesus strikes hard at pious pretension and self-righteousness, such as the Pharisee who prayed in public to advertise his own excellence. Luke's Jesus strikes hard at indifference to human suffering, such as that clergyman and that lawyer who turned their eyes away and hurried past on the other side of the road while an injured man lay groaning in the dirt. Luke's Jesus strikes hard at the refusal to forgive one who repents, such as the older brother who disclaimed any relationship to the returned prodigal.

Luke strikes hard at racial prejudice, such as the Jewish disdain for Samaritans, and he strikes hard at greed, such as the rich fool who stuffed his barn full of goodies as a hedge against inflation and then died the next night. Luke saw all these attitudes as diseases which could kill a person as surely as smallpox. And he saw Jesus as one who effectively assaulted them.

The Gospel of Luke overflows with compassion for the underdog. This Jesus was a friend of publicans and sinners. He came to seek and to save the lost. Luke's Gospel is the only one that holds women in high esteem and deals gently with their needs. You catch this in the opening idylls of Elizabeth, Mary, and Anna. You find it in the stories about the woman who was a sinner, Mary and Martha, the widow of Nain, and at the end of the book when Jesus gives his words of warning and consolation to the daughters of Jerusalem.

And, finally, it is a Gospel of joy. My children often come to me with their crayons and coloring book and ask, "Daddy, what color should I make this ball or wagon?"

I think if they asked me what color they should make the Gospel of Luke, I would say, "Color it joy!" Luke is a Gospel that sparkles and shines. At the beginning, Luke says, "I bring you news of a great joy . . ." In the middle, the father of the returned prodigal cries out, "Bring quickly the best robe . . . put a ring on his hand, and shoes on his feet; and bring the fatted calf. . . let us eat and make merry; for this my son was dead, and is alive again; he was lost and is found." And at the end of the Gospel there was gladness when the disciples met their risen Lord and "returned to Jerusalem with great joy . . ."

In a world continually torn open upon the jagged edge of war, and racked with the fevers of anxiety and insecurity, the Gospel of Luke is the kind of book that brings health and makes us whole persons in a broken world. It was Luke's wish that every human being come under the diagnostic gaze of the great Physician, sent by God to liberate the soul from the disfiguring power of sin, and make each one healthy and strong again as a member of the community where God's love reigns. This is what happened to Luke. His Gospel is an invitation to let it happen to us.

The Gospel of John
This is Eternal Life

John 3:14-17, 17:1-3

The four Gospels in the New Testament are the foundation blocks of our faith. They are the primary record of the life and ministry of our Lord Jesus Christ. We are examining these Gospels as total books this month. Each one has a major theme. Each one provides some special insight into the Master's personality. Each writer sees Jesus in a unique way.

Also, each book tells us something about the writer. Jesus touches each one in a special way and ministers to him at a point of his need. Thus, Mark, who was impatient to see inequalities righted, shows us a Jesus who was a man of action, striding through the world, doing battle with the forces of evil, and moving quickly to his appointment with the cross.

Matthew shows us a Jesus who is a noble teacher sent from God to instruct the world about God's mind for his creation. Jesus is the Messiah who fulfills Old Testament prophecy and law. Matthew writes for the young church. He sees it as the schoolroom of instruction where new Christians are nurtured, strengthened and sent out as witnesses to a weary world.

Luke writes for the diseased and maimed of this world. A physician himself, he sees Jesus as one who comes to heal the wounds of the world. Luke's Jesus assaults the cancerous attitudes of self-sufficiency and self-superiority — pride and prejudice — which can kill as surely as a sickness of the body. Luke's Gospel is compassionate toward the powerless and full of joy over the fact that at last they have a physician of the soul from God himself.

And then there is John. You do not have to read very far into the fourth Gospel to discover that you are treading on a ground different from that of the other three accounts. John is awesome ground — holy ground. It is written on two levels, the historical and the eternal. It is written in time, yet it takes you beyond time. The historical setting for Jesus' life and ministry in John is really a transparency through which we see timeless truth. This Gospel reminds me of a glass-bottom boat in which you experience two worlds at once.

John makes Jesus our contemporary who walks with us and helps us remain whole persons in a broken world. He makes our fellowship with God and each other immediate, intimate, and warm. John's Jesus reminds us that the Word made flesh still walks among us, and that there is not a day or circumstance in which he is not the Lord.

Who is this John who fills his pages, more than any other Gospel, with signs and sayings of Jesus announcing we have a genesis, an identity, and a destiny which reaches before and beyond this shutter-click of life and makes this historical instant of supreme and joyous significance?

Who is this John who records in minute detail the passion of our Lord from Palm Sunday to Easter and reproduces with photographic precision the emotional expressions of the disciples? What was his experience with Christ that caused him to write a life of Jesus which brings eternity into time, helping those who are bitter, who doubt and who grieve, to search out his words again and again for the strength to go on? Who is this John?

Well, let us see what we can discover about him. His name is common. There are five books in the New

Testament that bear the name, John: the gospel, three letters, and the Revelation. Our John did not write the Revelation. The use of the Greek language and the content of the two books are so radically different that there is almost unanimous opinion they are not from the same pen. But while the John of the Gospel knows Greek very well, he was probably a Jew. He betrays his Hebrew heritage through the use of idiom and his meticulous knowledge of the temple rituals and the procedures of the Jewish court called the Sanhedrin.

John writes late, more than seventy-five years after the crucifixion. The early church already had a foothold in the ancient world. Both Jews and non-Jews were members of this young church. But this church was being assaulted by the claims of the mystery religions, sect groups, and a renascence of Greek philosophy. The Christ of Matthew, Mark, and Luke was being twisted into unrecognizable form. It is John, so familiar with the intellectual temper of his time, who straightens out the record. Using the language and thought processes of the church's adversaries, he shows them who Christ truly is.

Finally, we might presume that John also gave us the three little letters in the New Testament, written in the twilight hours of his life and filled with gentleness and reflection upon that one great life which had gripped him and still waited to touch the new, untried lives of those who had yet to meet the master.

That may be all we can say with certainty, but we can speculate, too. I think John's Gospel betrays some deeper knowledge of his own need. I said that his book was written on two levels — the historical and the eternal. I think it was also written to be *read* on two levels. It can be read by those who meet Jesus as an historical personality for the first time. And it can be read by the devout Christian who wants to be led more deeply into communion with the living Lord.

John holds up Jesus as one who is like the ocean. On the one hand, he is as near and familiar as the bays and tides along the coast, friendly to boats and a source of life to fishermen. Yet, on the other hand, he is vast and unexplored, deep and mighty. Whether the reader is a skeptic or a devoted disciple, John says, "Come! This Jesus can stand any assault. He is the anvil upon which many hammers of doubt and despair are broken. I know, because I have been that route."

"Do you want to see me?" says John. "Then look at Philip who says, 'Lord, show us the Father, and we shall be satisfied.'

"Look at Thomas who says, 'Unless I see in his hands the print of the nails, and place my finger in the mark of the nails, and place my hand in his side, I will not believe.'

"Look at Nathanael who says, 'Can anything good come out of Nazareth?'

"Look at Peter who says, 'Lord, you know everything; you know that I love you.'

"Look at the nameless, beloved disciple who received into his care Christ's mother, who outran Peter to the empty tomb, saw and believed, and who said to Peter by the sea when Jesus appeared to them, 'It is the Lord!'

"Look at them all, reader. They are myself. They represent the journey of faith and unfaith I have taken. And look at them all, reader. They are you, also. These persons who walk with Jesus, who falter from him, deny him, believe in him, all represent our own pilgrimage and discovery of Jesus Christ as Lord and giver of eternal life."

John writes to encourage you and me to follow Jesus and grow in his presence. He projects himself into the personalities of the disciples, using on the one hand Thomas as skeptic and doubter, who says that seeing is believing, and on the other the beloved disciple who teaches us that believing is seeing. They represent the two poles of attitude with all the shades of disbelief and commitment in between, yet Jesus loves them both.

The major thrust of the Gospel of John is to lead us to eternal life. And it comes as a surprise to discover that eternal life is not merely a *quantity* of time that is ahead. It is a *quality* of life that is now. Eternal life is always cast in the present tense, and it is always tied tightly to belief. How does John say it?

For God so loved the world that he gave his only Son, that whoever believes in him should not perish but have eternal life. (John 3:16)

And this is eternal life, that they know thee the only true God, and Jesus Christ whom thou hast sent. (John 17:3)

The Gospel of John invites us to believe that God is the beginning, the process, and the ending of all things; to believe that love, which pours itself out for another, is the one thing that lasts forever. The Gospel of John invites us to believe that Jesus is God's fleshed-out word to a weary and fearful world, to believe that there are many rooms in the Father's house, and that he has a parent's plans for his creation. John invites us to live in the light of that kind of belief, and he assures us that it is in the living we find the proof we so desperately want.

This is eternal life; to take Christ at his word and get down to the business of living creatively and joyfully with other members of the Father's family who share both this planet and our pilgrimage with us between the times.

IV.

The

Great

Commandments

With All Your Heart

Deuteronomy 6:4-9

The basic way the Christian faith speaks about the relationship between God and human beings is love. We are taught that God loves us and that we can love God. What is not always clear is the order in which this mutual adoration takes place.

The Bible is quite precise in its description of love's initiative. It is God who loved us first. From the opening notes of creation, the entire symphony of biblical history is a recitation of God's actions toward us. The exodus, the covenant, the tribal confederation, the exile and return, the promise of the Messiah, the coming of Christ, and the birth and growth of the church are all seen as indicators of God's freely given love to his people. Our response is to be in kind.

It is our response in love to God's action of love that I wish to explore during the next few weeks. We are going to look carefully at a text which is most familiar to all of us — the two great commandments of Jesus.

These commandments appear in the first three Gospels. In Matthew and Luke, they are spoken by another in response to a question from Jesus. Only in Mark do the words come from the mouth of the Master. And only in Mark does Jesus preface the commandments with the great statement of faith of the Hebrew people:

Jesus answered, "The first is, 'Hear, O Israel: The Lord our God, the Lord is one; and you shall love the Lord your God with all your heart, and with all your soul, and with all your mind, and with all your strength.' The second is this, 'You shall love your neighbor as yourself.' There is no other commandment greater than these." (Mark 12:28-31)

The lesson from Deuteronomy today is the source for that statement of faith and for the first great commandment. Surely, these are words that Jesus knew well from his childhood: "Hear, O Israel: the Lord our God is one Lord." This preface can still be heard in every service of worship in the synagogue today in much the same way that we recite our Lord's prayer. And this preface is quite as important for the Christian as it is for the Jew, for if we believed in many gods, the total devotion required by the first great commandment would be impossible.

There are gods galore in our time just as there were in ancient Israel: money, social standing, political power, nature, youth. But this preface directs us to a matter of priority — the Lord our God is one. If we believe that, then we must demonstrate it — and you shall love the Lord with heart, soul, mind, and strength.

So then, this morning let's look at the first way of loving God — with all our hearts. Isn't it amazing the way the word "heart" occupies such a prominent place in our language? But the way we use it does not make much sense from a physiological point of view. The heart is a pump. It's action keeps us alive. That's all there is to it. Why do we persist, then, in making such statements as, "Have a heart," or "Let's get to the heart of the matter," or "My heart isn't in it," or "I have learned this by heart"?

I think we sense unconsciously that our passion for logic and scientific description does not always serve us well when it comes to matters of the spirit. An unscientific people such as the ancient Hebrews have much to teach us about the dimensions of the invisible and immeasurable.

In the Old Testament, more than eighty parts of the human body are named. Of this number, three organs became associated with intense emotional experience: the heart, the kidneys, and the bowels. And of these three the heart is most widely used for such expression. It expresses anxiety: "His heart trembled for the ark of God." (1 Samuel 4:13) It expresses joy: "Therefore my heart is glad." (Psalms 16:9) It expresses love; "The king's heart went out to Absalom." (2 Samuel 14:1) It even expresses intoxicated gaity; "Nabal's heart was merry within him, for he was very drunk." (1 Samuel 25:36)

Also, the heart was used to express mental activity, for there is no word for brain in the ancient Hebrew. The word "heart" deals with the inner life and character of persons, an inner life we can hide for a while from others, but which is always known to God. "The Lord said to Samuel, 'Man looks on the outward appearance, but the Lord looks on the heart.'" (1 Samuel 16:7)

In one of Dorothy Sayers' plays, the disciples are gathered with Jesus in the upper room. He tells them that one will betray him. Immediately, all the disciples ask, "Is it I?" They all feel indicted. It is Peter, however, who gives full voice to his feelings. He turns to one of his companions with the admission that Jesus must certainly be speaking about him for he knows he has many unswept, dusty corners in his heart which he would not even allow the Lord to see.

To love God with all your heart has about it a sense of self-searching honesty. It is a willingness to confess a self-knowledge of that which God knows about us. And by such a confession a relationship is restored, maintained, and nurtured.

When the Hebrew people went into exile, they went with crushed and desolate spirits. The prophet

Jeremiah ministered to them by writing pastoral letters of encouragement. In one of those letters, he says,

> For I know the plans I have for you, says the Lord, plans for welfare and not for evil, to give you a future and a hope. Then you will call upon me and come and pray to me, and I will hear you. You will seek me and find me; when you seek me with all your heart. (Jeremiah 29:11-13)

These were no empty words from a prophet who took his ease while others suffered. Jeremiah knew how difficult it was to stay on course in the midst of a struggle. He knew how many diversions there are to pull us away from the object of our search. To love God with all our hearts does not mean to withdraw from life so we won't be side-tracked in our search. Instead, it means to scan every experience in life for some confirmation of the holy in it, and for some way to use the experience to fulfill God's intentions of love.

To love God with all our heart requires self-honesty and confession, such as Peter's. It means to bear hope like Jeremiah, and see great value in another as did Jesus. To love God with all our hearts means to wear our heart on our sleeve, so that others can touch the center of our lives and feel the power of that to which we have committed ourselves.

The great commandment places heart first as a way of summing up the specifics that follow. The soul, the mind, and the strength are employed in the way the heart instructs them. If I love God with all my heart, then I have let the Almighty seize my life to be used by him. I can hide no longer. And even though I may burn my fingers a hundred times in the same fires of frailty, this Almighty One does not let me go. He leads me with patience and love to deal with others in the same way he has dealt with me.

With All Your Soul

Psalms 42
Matthew 11:28-30

We are exploring the two great commandments Jesus gives to us. They have to do with love of God and love of neighbor. They sum up the ten commandments received by Moses. However, unlike the law of Moses, they are not prohibitions. They are positive statements that lead us into an adventure of love.

The first great commandment teaches us of four ways to love God — with heart, soul, mind, and strength. Last week we looked at what it means to love with all your heart. We learned there is an emotional intensity in such a love. To love with the heart acknowledges that God knows what we deny about ourselves. Also it means to scan every experience, good or bad, for some confirmation of the holy in it.

This morning, Jesus instructs us to love the Lord with all our souls. The word "soul" is precious to us. It conveys a sense of hope beyond this mortal life. We speak of the immortality of the soul as if to say that when this body has finished its task, some indefinable essence will be released to take its place with God.

I recall hearing some time ago a most exceptional epitaph which expresses this thought in a light-hearted way. I believe it went something like this:
Here lies the body of Benjamin Pease,
Under the meadow, under the trees;
But Pease is not here, there's only the pod;
Pease is shelled and gone home to God.
Well, that's one way to think of yourself — as a

pea in a pod, and that the final act of life is to strip off the outer nature in order to reveal the inner, authentic reality. However, I have a two-fold quarrel with that idea. First, must I wait for death to disclose the real? And second, is my bodily life to be disregarded as an authentic vessel for the expression of God's activity?

We think too much like the ancient Greeks in our contemplation of ourselves and not enough like the ancient Hebrews. The Greeks viewed the body as a prison for the soul. Life was a struggle to set it free for its reunion with God. The Hebrew was not so speculative, not dualistic. He did not divide himself up into the earthly and the heavenly. He thought of himself on a physical level almost exclusively.

The word "soul" had its beginning in the Old Testament as a term meaning little more than a living being who breathes. In the creation story, God blows the breath of life into the nostrils of Adam and he becomes a living soul. The word is also used in the Old Testament for physical appetite, distress, desire, and life. The last word, "life," is perhaps the best translation, for it is the soul that gives wholeness to the human frame. It is the fourth dimension, after the emotions, mind, and body, which completes the creature and makes us human. It is the animating quality which makes life with God possible and knowable.

In the New Testament the word for soul is translated from the Greek word *psyche*. This is where we get our word "psychology." No English translation can do it justice. Psyche also means life, but it means more than physical life and something other than psychological self. It's something you feel in every fibre of your being. As we handle the circumstances of life and the materials of the world, the conviction comes that the soul is of a different order other from the stuff of which the earth is made.

The Christian faith steadfastly affirms the importance of both the outer world and the inner world — the senses and the soul. The outer world is a work of God and is the environment for his many blessings. But the inner world is marked by God with the seal of his intentions. The soul serves to give meaning to all the things God has made. This function brings God very close to us — closer than hands and feet.

People are threatened and their faith is assaulted by every new scientific discovery that expands the size and complexity of the universe. God becomes so big and distant that they feel forsaken.

Centuries ago, Galileo was accused of moving God too far away from people with his discoveries about the universe. Galileo's inner world of the soul answered these accusations by discussing the meaning of this outer world discovery as a sign of God's creative activity. He indicated that the sun, which has all those planets revolving about it, and dependent upon it for their orderly functions, could also ripen a bunch of grapes on the vine as if it had nothing else in the world to do. By the same token, God is able to tend us as if he had nothing else in the world to do.

This kind of over-arching care by the Almighty was good news to the Psalmist who held conversation with his soul as he tried to find a way through the anxieties and loneliness of life. It was good news to the prodigal son who sat with the swine in a distant land, contemplating his miserable condition brought on by his misuse of freedom. And it's good news to you and me who wonder about direction as we are tossed about like corks in the sea by the powerful currents of the modern world. God keeps us all as if we were his only partners in the universe, and animates our lives with soul-power to send us on missions of meaning.

But we have to use our souls, just as we do our minds and bodies. They have a capacity for growth also. Many people overlook that fact. Some think the soul is just there from birth, mature and waiting, like a check made payable to the bearer in terms of salvation. All you have to do is be morally decent, join the church, and acknowledge some kind of heavenly power in order to endorse the check and reap its benefits. Beyond this initial acknowledgment, nothing else is done. The soul is put to bed before it has a chance to stretch its muscles and greet the dawn. The soul needs exercise, training and challenge. This is what Philip Doddridge indicates in his hymn:

Awake, my soul, stretch every nerve,
And press with vigor on;
A heavenly race demands thy zeal,
And an immortal crown.

We have to let our souls run loose and free and lead us into places we have never been before — into some new situation, some new relationship. It may be risky, we may feel uncomfortable, we may say the wrong thing. But Jesus once remarked that it is better to go into life with a broken leg, or a crippled arm, than to live in the cramped dimensions of the fearful and the timid.

Also, we have to let our souls drink deeply from the small and humble pools of life's experience rather than from just the mighty cataracts. We worship too much before the spectacular. We grovel before success and the influential. We're fond of saying, "I know so and so," never realizing that its not who you know that counts, but who knows you.

It's God who knows you and comes to meet you in the most seemingly insignificant ways — in a burning bush, as a voice in the night, at a potter's wheel, as a prisoner or a hungry person, and through a cattle crib in a Bethlehem barn. God humbles himself so we can meet him as a friend. Our problem is that we try to exalt ourselves so we can reach him, and we miss him.

Again, give your soul credit for its own uniqueness. Don't dress it up in someone else's piety. Say your own prayers in the language of your own joy. Thank God for what has given you happiness even though no one else would think it worthy to mention.

For the sake of order and function we have forms in our church life and worship to help us move forward together. But God forbid that these forms become so rigid that there is no room for the expression of different souls. There is no way by which one person can insinuate the God experience upon another person's life. God will come into that life as he came into ours, by a mysterious, inward, intimate, individual invasion that defies our ideas of conformity.

You shall love the Lord your God with all your soul. What is this but the acknowledgment that God has placed a restlessness within us that finds no rest until it locates itself in him. And this can surely happen, not just at the end of life, but in the midst of life, and not at the expense of the body with all its glory, but by using the body as its means of expression.

Jesus told us to come to him when we labor and are heavy-laden and he will give rest for our souls. He asks us to take his yoke upon us — a yoke that is easy and a burden that is light. This is not an invitation to retire from life, nor is the rest he offers the rest of slackness. When we follow his leading seriously, we take on more burdens than ever before. The promise is that he never gives us more than we can carry, and he teaches us how to adjust the load. The rest that comes to the soul is the relief of having, finally, a direction for our mind and strength so that we can complete the charge of the great commandment.

To love God with the heart and soul is a command to address ourselves to our inner lives — to find out who we are and to whom we belong. Only then are we able to address ourselves to the outer life of mind and strength and finally participate with God in leading others out of their orphan-mood back into the family.

With All Your Mind

Philippians 2:1-13

This month we are examining together the great commandments of Jesus. He helps us direct our devotional energies by spelling out the ways we can love God and love our neighbor. In the first great commandment he indicates that we shall love God with our hearts, souls, minds, and strength.

For the past two weeks we looked at the meaning of heart and soul. They have to do with the inner life — the secret place of confession and decision, of promise and preparation. But while the love of God with heart and soul is an inner experience, it can never be a totally isolated, invisible exercise. The inward posture must complete itself in outward expression. The heart and soul provide the foundation upon which we love God with mind and strength.

This morning, then, let us explore the Lord's command to love God with our minds. In the Old Testament source for this commandment in Deuteronomy the word "mind" is not used. For the ancient Hebrew the heart was the seat of intellect as well as the source of emotional activity and feeling. There is no word for brain in Hebrew.

By the time the New Testament was written, the use of the Greek language separated the activities of intellect and emotion. In the New Testament, the mind had to do with thought. Christians have the capacity to direct their intellects in the enterprise of the faith. There are great facts to learn and great ideas to discuss on this pilgrimage of love.

A visitor to a country town went to the local political rally where the aspiring candidate for office was speaking. This visitor sat next to a man who shouted at and applauded every statement the speaker made regardless of its relevancy or logical consistency. Each comment called for a vocal ejaculation of some kind. When the speaker finished his address, the visitor turned to his verbal neighbor and asked, "Well, what did you think of the speech?"

The man turned and looked the stranger up and down for a moment and then replied, "Mister, I didn't come here to think. I came here to holler!"

I shudder when that kind of remark is made in the church community. "I didn't become a Christian to think, or to learn. I don't want to struggle with eternal truths. I don't want to be a Christian in process; I want to be a Christian in a cocoon where I can rest on Sunday morning and let things float over me. Out there in the world my brain spins all the time from the signals that are beamed at me. I want some peace and quiet in the church!"

The church does offer the glorious possibility of encountering the peace, the *shalom*, of God. But shalom is not the peace of escape or slackness. If you want that, take the phone off the hook and soak in a hot tub for an hour. The shalom of God does not invite us to let our mental tackle hang loose. It is the kind of peace that allows us to hear truths and discuss ideas we've been too busy to hear and discuss at other times. And rather than leave these truths and ideas here after the benediction, we are enjoined to take them out with us into that rough and tumble world and use them to move through and overcome the confusions that assault us.

On her day off, the old washer woman would go into the movie theater at one o'clock in the afternoon and sit through showing after showing of the main feature. At ten o'clock in the evening when the last film was done, she would sit there and weep over the fact that there was not another picture. The ushers gently led her out, nodding sympathetically to her protests of why the world could not be as lovely as the picture show.

And we are led out, too, whenever we come to this place of worship. We cannot stay here. We must go, but hopefully we do so armed with resources to redeem our lives. Some of these resources are intellectual ones. Our faith demands mental reflection. There are many hard teachings in the Gospels. Even the disciples said that very thing to Jesus. "Master, this is a hard teaching."

Jesus and his disciples often discussed his teachings together. There was conflict and disagreement. There was misunderstanding. But there are also recorded instances when the disciples stretched their minds and understood what this strange man had to do with them. Who can forget Peter's ringing affirmation, "You are the Christ, the Son of the living God." (Matthew 16:16)

There once was a preacher who took pride in the fact that he never prepared his sermons for public worship. He said that the Holy Spirit always gave him utterance in the pulpit each Sunday morning. Indeed, the Spirit does empower us all in the most surprising ways to speak and act, even when we feel we are unable to do so. But one day he took his place to deliver the sermon, offered a prayer, and opened his mind for the invasion of the Spirit. He waited and waited until finally a still, small voice came to him, saying, "My son, thou art unprepared this morning!"

Even the Spirit must have fertile, tilled ground in which to plant the seeds of truth. We are to love the Lord our God with our minds. We must prepare ourselves to converse intelligently with the many competing systems of belief in our world. We are all scholars in Christ. This does not mean we must have a

PhD, or go to a theological seminary. We do not all need to possess the same breadth of intellectual gifts. That would make the church a tedious fellowship. There is a wide spectrum of mental agility in every congregation. All of us are enriched by each of us as we share our insights together.

Love the Lord your God with all your minds! That command asks many things of our minds. But the one thing above all it asks is that we take seriously the book of faith, our Bible. It is the textbook of the Christian fellowship. In it we first meet Jesus Christ as an historical figure. We have to meet him that way first before he can meet us as an ever-present companion. Soon, however, the Bible moves from being a textbook to becoming a drama. The suspense heightens. The facts become faces. You move to the edge of your seat. Finally, you leave your seat and go on stage. The Bible becomes a drama about you and me.

The church is a learning community. We tell stories to each other. We have to use our minds to get the story straight before we can get the story in and get the story out.

Every church is made up of a great variety of people. Members do not all think the same; their priorities are different. But on one issue they must be of one mind. Paul says it this way: "Have this mind among yourselves which you have in Christ Jesus . . ." He then recites the mystery of the incarnation — how God became a human being and lived with us in humility and obedience, died and was raised. Have this mind, so that every tongue will confess that Jesus Christ is Lord, to the glory of God the Father! The goal of mind employment is to achieve a mindset about God in Christ. He is Lord!

As we use our minds in this enterprise, we will encounter mysteries that require us to take a leap of faith and say, "I believe." No human mind is totally adequate to comprehend the height and depth, the breadth of God's love. Our minds are one more tool among many given by God to move into his presence. And as we come to the threshold, he puts out his hand and asks us to step over in trust in the same way a child steps out into a busy street holding the hand of a parent, confident that no harm will come. It is that act of reaching out beyond the threshold that leads us to finally say with assurance, "Now I really know!"

> *Heart and mind, possessions, Lord, I offer unto thee;*
> *All these were thine, Lord; thou didst give them all to me.*
> *Wondrous are thy doings unto me.*
> *Plans and my thoughts and everything I ever do are dependent on thy will and love alone.*
> *I commit my spirit unto thee.*

With All Your Strength

Philippians 3:7-16

We are looking at the great commandments during these weeks. It is a good instruction for those who look for the meaning of love of God and of neighbor. It is a way to give thanks and sing praise to God who shows his care for us by supporting the world in which we live, and by confronting us with a human being who speaks God's will in a language we can understand — the language of birth and struggle, friendship and teaching, weeping and laughter, and even death.

We love God because he first loved us. Jesus suggests four ways to do this: with heart and soul, with mind and strength. The first great commandment asks us to pay attention to our endowments of emotion and spirit, intellect and dexterity. They are gifts with a potential for growth. We have to use what we have been given, lest the gifts wither and lead to bitterness and despair.

The great commandment has both internal and external elements about it. The heart and soul reflect the inner life of emotional intensity, self-honesty, and a sense of eternity. They are the engines that drive the outer life reflections of mind and strength.

Today, we are looking at the last way to love God — with all your strength. The word "might," or "strength," is quite straightforward. In both Testaments it has a sense of muscle power about it. It has to do with hands and feet, with labor and physical energy. It has to do with the facility of the human body to get things done.

In our text, Paul talks about the single-minded,

energetic devotion with which he pursues the upward call of God in Christ Jesus. He uses language that has a physical dynamism about it. Like a sprinter who leaves the mark at the sound of the gun, he does not look behind, but strains forward to what lies ahead. He presses on toward the goal for the prize that awaits him there.

Now, as you contemplate these images, it is interesting to discover that some scholars have suggested that Paul may have had physical limitations. Some indicate he was frail. There is evidence he was accompanied on his journeys by a physician, Dr. Luke. Some have even been so bold as to say he was an epileptic. We shall probably never know. But if such speculation has a good word to say to us, it is that to love God with all your strength does not mean you have to run a mile under four minutes, pitch a no-hitter, or out-skate Dorothy Hammel. That would leave just about all of us out and cause us to despair. The implication is that we are to channel what strength we have, and the talents we possess, in creative ways within the limits of our endurance.

I remember reading about a famous university professor who learned something about strength in the last days of his life. As his physical powers decreased, he could work only an hour a day at his desk, then a half hour, and then twenty minutes. But into those twenty minutes of physical endurance and mental activity he compressed a day's work. Not that he could accomplish as much, for the time was not there. But some time was there and some physical strength was there. And he used it creatively and intensely. He said, "These twenty minutes comprise my day. As long as I have that day, I am alive and well."

We all have strength to love our God. We all have talents to offer at the altar of praise. We dare not let our limitations deter us and cause us to weep over what used to be. That leads to spiritual paralysis. Let us be thankful for what is and what we can do.

Here is an example: Not long ago, little children brought food and gifts to church for people in town and for Christian Community Action in the city of New Haven. Young people sorted, packed, and loaded these items into boxes and cars. Middle-aged people drove them to their destinations and unloaded them. And elderly people wrote letters and notes of love and joy indicating that these were thank-offerings to God who gave us all the strength to share. All different forms of strength-employment covering the entire life cycle, yet with only one goal: to love the Lord our God with all our strength.

But now, something is happening to this first great commandment. Even though it is intensely personal in its thrust, it is beginning to spill over into an area that is intensely social. Another voice is beginning to be heard — the voice of our neighbors around us. To love God with all your strength leads us to step out on a bridge that moves us into another dimension. The strength we have in our bodies almost always expresses itself in a way that touches the life of another human being. There is an ancient legend that speaks to this transition.

The Christ child was walking through the world. He came to a river, wide and swift, over which he could not pass. Seated on the bank of the river was a giant whose name was Reprobatus (from which we get our word, reprobate). The Christ child asked the giant to carry him across the river. Reprobatus grumbled at this request, but seeing one so wistful and so pure, a spark was kindled deep that led him to agree.

He lifted the child and placed him on his back, wondering at the weight of the infant. He waded into the river, struggling under his burden. When he reached the other side, Reprobatus placed the child on the ground and fell exhausted to the earth. When he could speak, he looked at the Christ child and asked, "How is it that one so small can be so heavy?"

The child replied, "Because I carry with me the sins of the world. But now, I shall give you a new name. No longer shall you be called Reprobatus. You shall be called Christopher, because you have carried Christ."

Whenever we say we will use our energies to praise God and Christ — our hearts, souls, minds, and strength — we are at the same time taking upon our shoulders the sins and sufferings of the world, for this is what God did in Jesus. When we say we have God in our hearts, or in our minds, or that we'll bend our strength for God, we are carrying the world along with us, and that is quite a load! The first great commandment is incomplete and virtually impossible without the second: You shall love your neighbor as yourself.

The first great commandment is a statement of faith that says, "I believe in God." We do not understand his ways completely, nor see him fully. But we have heard enough of his word and seen enough of his work to believe that more than blind chance and self-interest motivates the world. This is the burden Jesus bore for God and for us.

We are drawn by Christ's posture. We want to know his secret. We want to see people the way he did. But in order to do that, we have to see God as he did; as one who loves the world, not because it can be trusted, but because it is of great worth. When we recognize and accept that we are loved that way, then we can see and accept other people in the same way.

To love God with heart, soul, mind, and strength leads to a semicolon in life, not to a period that ends the sentence. The words that follow the first great commandment are the ones that complete the thought in the mind of God. You shall love your neighbor as yourself. These words of the Apostle Peter lead us into the second great commandment:

Above all hold unfailing your love for one another, since love covers a multitude of sins. Practice hospitality ungrudgingly to one another. As each has received a gift, employ it for one another, as good stewards of God's varied grace: whoever speaks, as one who utters oracles of God; whoever renders service, as one who renders it by the strength which God supplies; in order that in everything God may be glorified through Jesus Christ. To him belong glory and dominion for ever and ever. Amen. (1 Peter 4:8-11)

Our Neighbors and Ourselves

Leviticus 19:11-18
Luke 10:25-37

Over the past four weeks we have examined the first great commandment. Jesus reminds us of what the Hebrew people first discovered: that the Lord our God is one Lord, not many, and that our total devotion is to be toward him. To say that I love the Lord my God with all my heart, my soul, my mind and strength, is the same as saying, "To you, O Lord, I commit my life."

But there is a second commandment also. You shall love your neighbor as yourself. Jesus says this is great, too. The two great commandments are bound together. Separated from each other, each is incomplete.

To love God and not your neighbor is essentially *hypocritical*, for it is God who has loved both you and your neighbor into life and bound you in kinship with each other. To hate your neighbor is to break up the family.

And to love your neighbor and not God is essentially *hopeless*, for such love degenerates into a mutual trembling together in the face of approaching darkness. All we can do is feed each other in despair until the food runs out. Such love bravely wrings a shallow joy from the moment, yet always feels the winds of oblivion howling up ahead.

The source of the second great commandment is found in the book of Leviticus. It is part of a large section embracing ten chapters called the Holiness Code. At first glance, this Holiness Code looks like a disconnected collection of laws about animal slaughter, eating and grooming habits, sexual conduct, and general morality. Yet, one word ties it all together — the word "holy." To be holy in the Hebrew sense is not to be saintly or perfect as we sometimes understand it. To be holy has to do with being set apart. It means to be uncommon.

The phrase, "I am the Lord," appears at least fifty times in this code. Its repetition indicates that the holy, uncommon God has chosen a people and set before them the charge to be holy — to be uncommon and set apart for a special task. These laws reflect that process. And one of these laws is to love your neighbor as yourself.

Now, to deal honestly with this text in Leviticus, we must recognize that this commandment had a limited application. The word "neighbor" had the root meaning of "friend" or "kinsman." To be holy by loving your neighbor referred primarily to the nation of Israel. It did not necessarily include the foreigner or traveler in the land.

It is Jesus who casts this second great commandment into a universal mode. He breaks down the creedal, ethnic, racial, and national boundaries that surround it. This is made clear in the lesson from Luke where the commandment is recited, not by Jesus, but by a lawyer.

The lawyer asks the Lord what he must do to inherit eternal life. This could be a sincere question, but the text indicates it is a trap to discredit Jesus. Sensing this, Jesus throws the question back, "What do you read in the law?"

This barrister of the faith recites his answer flawlessly. After all, that's his business.

Jesus, then, responds in a way to cut off the conversation, "Absolutely correct! Go and do this, and you will live!"

Well, the lawyer is flustered by this dismissal.

Unwilling to let the matter go, he sticks his foot in his mouth and asks another question that is his undoing — or could it be his salvation — "And who is my neighbor?"

What follows is so familiar to us, it scarcely bears repeating. Jesus tells a story about a Samaritan who is a traveler in the land. Samaritans were considered to be enemies of the Jews. Yet, Jesus tells of one who had compassion upon a Jew in distress, and who loves him with a love he would not receive were the situation reversed. At the end of the story, Jesus asks the question our world still has not come to terms with: Who was neighbor to the one in trouble?

The lawyer had no choice but to swallow his nationalistic, religious, and racial pride and answer, "The one who showed mercy."

Jesus' final statement ends the interrogation, "You go and do the same whenever the occasion presents itself."

There is a question we must always ask ourselves whenever we are confronted with another human being: How do we regard ourselves? If we think that we are self-superior, then we cannot grant this stature to our neighbor, for there can only be one "King of the mountain" — Me!

If we view ourselves as self-sufficient, then we will not make contact with our neighbor, for we do not need him, nor do we feel that he needs us. Self-sufficiency does not allow personhood to come to full flower.

And if we consider ourselves to be worthless, then the exhaustion born out of self-pity leaves no energy to reach out and touch our neighbor. After all, what's the use? Vanity of vanities, all is vanity.

To love yourself after the manner of the second great commandment is to believe that you are of great worth to God, that you are sustained, and that his faithfulness has been directed toward you, even when you have been unfaithful. This godly sense of worth is most commonly mediated through other people who stick by us when we want to give up, and who forgive us when our teeth are set on edge.

To love yourself is to discover that you are loved, and that you dare not break the chain letter by failing to share that love with another in the same way it was communicated to you. This is what Paul means when he says that a Christian is a letter from Christ. (2 Corinthians 3:1-3) The message does not get through until you are opened and read by another.

Long ago the Psalmist sat out on a hillside at night and, looking at the vastness of the sky, thought about himself in relation to the universe. He said to himself something like this:

What is man that thou shouldst love him,
Creature that thy hand hath made?
Child of earth, yet full of yearning,
Mixture strange of good and ill,
From thy ways so often turning,
Yet thy love doth seek him still. *

That is who I am, and that is who my neighbor is. And the Lord has loved us both into life to live together. We come here every week to praise God, to feel his forgiveness, and to offer him the best we have. We come here in the spirit of the first great commandment. Sometimes we wonder if it is always necessary that our neighbor intrude upon our thoughts. Can't that neighbor who has caused us aggravation all week long stay out of the picture for just these few moments? No, the neighbor will not stay out of the picture. Every time we lift our eyes from prayer and try to see the cross, there, in the

---

*Reprinted by permission from "Oh How Glorious, Full of Wonder" by Curtis Beach. Copyright 1958 by the Pilgrim Press.

think just holy thoughts in worship. His or her presence tests our words against our actions. We are to see our neighbor as one whom God loves and for whom Christ died.

In the parable of the good Samaritan, Jesus was essentially saying to the lawyer, "Look! You have asked the wrong question. It is not 'Who is my neighbor?' That kind of question looks for a limit. It only looks for a time when you can stop loving your neighbor and feel good about it. The right question is this, 'To whom should I be a neighbor?' You are to be a neighbor to all."

At this point Jesus goes beyond the Holiness Code of Leviticus, which attempted to catalogue all conceivable human situations and their limits. For Christ, the possibilities for relationship are infinite.

The second great commandment does not ask us to make people love us. All it asks is that we be poised and ready at a moment's notice, to take up the burden of a neighbor in the same way we would want our neighbor to respond to our need.

I really cannot think about God without thinking about my neighbor and myself, for we two are apparent to each other more of the time than is God. And that is God's secret and surprising way with us — that we discover and marvel in his presence with us when we enter upon a life of concern for each other.

When we worship, we gaze inward upon ourselves and take a sounding of our commitment to God and Christ. And as we look we see Jesus who came to be our neighbor as well as to be our God. Rejected by men, he illustrates in his flesh and blood the parable of the good Samaritan. He does not ask if we are his neighbor. He acts as neighbor. He does for us what, in faith, he believes we will do for others.

Where cross the crowded ways of life,
Where sound the cries of race and clan,

way, is the shadow of our neighbor, obscuring what we want to see, until we see our neighbor first.

Our neighbor will not let us talk just holy talk, or
Above the noise of selfish strife,
We hear thy voice, O Son of man. *

Does my neighbor hear that voice in my dealings with him? In fact, can he really hear it any other way?